Esther or Delilah?

Esther or Delilah?

ANGELA DE SOUZA

Tales of Beauty & Seduction

An honest look at how women use their beauty to seduce men! Whether you like it or not you are using your beauty for something, but are you using it to **empower** a man or are you using it in a way that leaves him **powerless**? Both Esther and Delilah were beautiful women in the Bible. Both women seduced the man in their life. One woman used her beauty to save her people; the other woman used her beauty to destroy her people. Today's women are no different from Esther and Delilah.

Which woman are you?

Copyright © 2012 by Angela De Souza

ALL RIGHTS RESERVED

No part of this book may be reproduced, stored in a retrieval system, or transmitted, in any form or by any means – electronic, mechanical, photocopying, recording or otherwise – without prior written permission.

ISBN-13:   978-1466372542

ISBN-10:   1466372540

BISAC: FAM029000

           Family & Relationships / Love & Romance

Contents

Introduction 1

Esther's Story 3

Delilah's Story 25

Esther or Delilah? 33

Influence 53

Respect 65

Submission 75

Favour 99

Timing 109

If I Perish, I Perish 115

Ruth's Story 133

Jezebel's Story 141

Ruth or Jezebel? 151

Patience 163

Gentleness 169

Abigail's Story 175

Courage 183

Faithfulness 193

Proverbs 31 205

Introduction

Introduction

Men were made to be **strong**: I don't see women in the bible killing giants, killing bears or throwing themselves in a pit on a snowy day to kill a lion. Women were designed to be **beautiful**.

Today's women are confused because they know they were designed for something special, they know God made them with a specific purpose and they know that it's something big that they are called to do! Deep down inside every woman feels this call to greatness but few women figure out what to do with it - and so instead we try to be strong. We try and assert ourselves in our workplace, in our homes and in our communities. We try and be who we think we should be. We grow stronger but can't seem to find satisfaction.

The reason for this, I believe, is because we are going about it the wrong way. We were not made to be strong with the strength of a man! Our strength is in our gentleness, our power lies in our beauty! Women were made to beautiful and those that know how to use their **beauty** can save nations.

M2M Men, there is a woman operating in your life. Perhaps you don't realise it but there is. She is either one of the two women we will refer to in this book – she is either an Esther or a Delilah. She is either beautifully bringing out your potential as a man of God or she is secretly seducing you to rob you of your strength.

She **is** operating - don't be fooled, so take careful note of how she operates and identify the woman that is influencing you. She may be your wife, girlfriend, mother, daughter, sister, pastor or friend. She is either good for you so embrace her, thank her and honour her; or she is bad for you, in this case run from her quickly, don't allow her to seduce you and rob you of your power any longer. Throughout this book I have placed some gems for you, wherever you see the M2M sign (Message 2 Men) you will find a section with keys especially for you - honest keys, things that most girls don't usually admit. I humbly make myself vulnerable so that these keys can help you take back the power that women are trying to steal from you.

Esther's Story

Esther's Story

A long, long time ago, in a country called Persia, there lived a powerful king named Ahasuerus (aHa-shoo-eerus). He ruled over a vast empire of one hundred and twenty seven provinces which spread all the way from India to Ethiopia. He ruled in his magnificent fortified palace along with his a beautiful, dazzling queen, Queen Vashti.

During his reign, King Ahasuerus wanted to show off to his entire kingdom, so he held the most spectacular, magnificent, awe inspiring feast. *He showed the riches of his glorious kingdom and the splendour of his excellent majesty for many days, one hundred and eighty days in all*[1]. Wine and other exotic drinks flowed without measure to all who attended. Food was delightful and plentiful. Entertainment

Esther or Delilah?

of the highest professional quality was provided. No expense was spared at the king's party. Yet, at the end of his extravagant feast, it seemed that the king's need to display his power was not satisfied. He proclaimed another feast; this one was for every single person in the county, *from great to small, in the court of the garden of the king's palace*[2].

Still, despite all the pompous parading and self-important showing off, he didn't seem to be satisfied. King Ahasuerus had a bright idea, an idea that would certainly be the cherry on top of the cake, an idea that would prove to all whom he ruled, that he was indeed the most powerful, most awesome king ever! He called for his queen. She was a beautiful queen, well groomed and something of a delight to behold. She was his possession and his bright idea was to show her off too, so that all could marvel at how rich and blessed the king was. The king sent seven of his finest men, *to show her beauty to the people and the officials, for she was beautiful to behold.* But Queen Vashti refused to come at the king's command brought by his eunuchs; therefore the king was furious, and his anger burned within him[3].

Anger coupled with confusion left the king baffled. He had not anticipated this. Was she even allowed to refuse him? Surely not! Unsure of what to do next, he asked his wise council; "What shall we do to Queen Vashti, according

Esther's Story

to law, because she did not obey the command of King Ahasuerus brought to her by the eunuchs?"[4]

One of the King's top men, Memucan, answered; "Queen Vashti has not only wronged the king, but also all the princes, and all the people who are in all the provinces of King Ahasuerus. For the queen's behaviour will become known to all women, so that they will despise their husbands in their eyes, when they report, 'King Ahasuerus commanded Queen Vashti to be brought in before him, but she did not come.' This very day the noble ladies of Persia and Media will say to all the king's officials that they have heard of the behaviour of the queen. Thus there will be excessive contempt and wrath.

If it pleases the king, let a royal decree go out from him, and let it be recorded in the laws of the Persians and the Medes, so that it will not be altered, that Vashti shall come no more before King Ahasuerus; and let the king give her royal position to another who is better than she.

When the king's decree which he will make is proclaimed throughout all his empire (for it is great), all wives will honour their husbands, both great and small."

And the reply pleased the king and the princes, and the king did according to the word of Memucan.[5] The king, heavily under the influence of much wine and feasting, decreed that Vashti was out. Banished. A new queen was to be chosen. His ego was bruised and his pride downtrodden under the harsh rejection of his queen. He walked off to his chamber sulking, not like a king but as a naughty school boy would. What a blow that must have been, his bright idea failed and all the months of feasting were quickly forgotten.

Questions plagued his mind. How would his subjects view him now? Would this outrageous action undermine his authority for all time? Was it to be written in the history books that King Ahasuerus was the laughing stock of his entire kingdom on this disastrous day? It was final, the decree was set in stone, even if the king wanted to change his mind now; he couldn't, the law in Persia was unchangeable. Once it had been written it could not be altered, even by the king himself.

Some time passed and the King's anger died down. He became lonely, bored perhaps. His thoughts drifted towards better times, times that included a beautiful woman, Vashti. His mind filled with thoughts of her soft skin, her beautiful face and her hands that used to touch him and bring him delight. His heart ached, longing for intimacy with a woman. His face drooped and his countenance became dull. It wasn't long before all who knew him could see plainly that something needed to be done for the king. His joy had left him and the days of feasting would be a distant memory for

Esther's Story

all if they did not cheer him up. *The king's servants who attended him said: "Let beautiful young virgins be sought for the king; and let the king appoint officers in all the provinces of his kingdom, that they may gather all the beautiful young virgins to the palace, into the women's quarters, under the custody of Hegai the king's eunuch, custodian of the women. And let beauty preparations be given to them. Then let the young woman who pleases the king be queen instead of Vashti."*

This thing pleased the king, and he did so.[6] Many beautiful virgins were prepared for him. Persia was in turmoil, a terrifying and delightful time for families with a young virgin or two. The town centre was filled with young girls with heavy makeup, wearing their best dress and high heels, all dressed up and standing around in the hope of being picked as the next queen. Meanwhile other women were in hiding. At home with their loved ones they hoped never to be discovered. Many virgins were already in love and hoping to be betrothed to the man of their dreams. The thought of palace life frightened them. Other girls simply didn't want to leave the comfort of their mother and father's home, so they hid too.

The whole region was in turmoil as word got out that the king was taking virgins to his palace. At one humble home,

Esther or Delilah?

soldiers began beating at the door. Each knock made Esther's heart leap and each knock made Mordecai more fearful. Esther was a beautiful, gracious and kind woman despite her difficult start in life. Her parents died when she was young leaving her an orphan at an early age. Mordecai, her older cousin, took her in and raised her as his daughter. Together they lived as Jews in Persia.

The knocking continued and gradually grew into harsh bashing, at which point Mordecai knew that they would not pass by and would rather break the door down than leave him alone.

Click.

No sooner had the latch slid upwards, than in burst the soldiers. Wrestling and protesting, Esther was taken to the palace for the king. She had no choice in the matter, it was as if she was stolen from her cousin and taken prisoner. She was removed from the only family she had left and was going to have to have sex with the king, just so that he could decide if he wanted her of not. Not a very nice position, yet she showed a great attitude to all the challenges that were thrown her way.

Mordecai was out of Esther's life for the time being and Hegai was to be her new master. She was sent to her new quarters, along with many other virgins, and lived as a royal

Esther's Story

slave. Royal because she had all the luxuries and wonderful delights of the palace, slave because she had no choice in the matter. Hegai remained in charge of the young virgins and Esther became the apple of his eye. She pleased him in a very pure way and she obtained his favour. Hegai was so pleased with her in fact, that he gave her extra beauty preparations, over and above what he gave to all the other virgins and besides her usual allowance. She was also given seven choice maidservants, the best maidservants available from the king's palace and then to top it all off nicely, he moved her and her maidservants to the best place in the house of the women. Esther, enjoying all the pampering and attention, had not revealed her people or family to anyone at all. Mordecai had charged her not to reveal it and she continued to respect Mordecai's wishes even though he no longer had contact with her.

It was a warm evening that evening. It was the evening that she would go from being a virgin to being a wife. This particular evening would change her life forever. This evening could even be the evening that the king chose his queen. But no matter what happened, once she had sex with the king, it was a done deal and she would be one of his wives. This evening was her wedding night to one of the most powerful men in the world. It was a warm evening

Esther or Delilah?

because she chose to feel the warmth of it rather than the coldness of it.

Either she would resent that she was being forced into a marriage and might possibly have to spend the remainder of her life in the king's harem as one of his many wives, never to be touched by a man again, or she could see the positives, in that no matter what happened to her, God would be with her always and bless her no matter what her circumstances turned out to be. Esther was at peace, she knew her God and she trusted Him with her life.

On that night, her wedding night to the king, *she was given whatever she desired to take with her from the women's quarters to the king's palace.*[7] Law stated that she had to be given any additional item of clothing or jewellery or anything at all that she wanted to make her more appealing to the king. Some girls requested musicians, roses and candles to enhance their wedding night. Others chose extra makeup and super sexy clothing. Some opted for food so that they could please the king's stomach first and afterwards move onto the king's other desires. The virgins only had one night with the king to win his favour.

One night.

One chance to make enough of an impression on the king. This impression was essential so that she would be

Esther's Story

remembered sufficiently to be called upon again on another night. Some women saw the king only once and were never seen by him again. They lived as widows in the king's harem, forgotten and unwanted. Most virgins would do whatever they could do to look beautiful so that they would be remembered. Esther was a beautiful woman who had undergone one year of beauty treatments in preparation for this one night. She remained at peace.

Now when the turn came for Esther..., to go in to the king, she requested nothing but what Hegai, advised. And Esther obtained favour in the sight of all who saw her.[8] She went to meet the King without any accessories, with nothing to offer him except herself. Esther walked into his chamber a virgin and left his chamber a wife. She left not knowing how she had performed. She left uncertain of what her future held. She walked out of his chamber and into her uncertain future.

Did the king remember her? Yes, he did. In fact, he was besotted with her. The king was smitten and was certain that he wanted to see Esther again. Perhaps it was her simplicity that caused the king to remember her or the lack of desperation on her part to be queen. Perhaps it was her tenderness, her gentle nature that won his heart? All of these things are probable but what we know for sure is that the King's favour stayed with her as *the king loved Esther*

 Esther or Delilah?

more than all the other women, and she obtained grace and favour in his sight more than all the virgins; so he set the royal crown upon her head and made her queen instead of Vashti[9].

This line could easily read, 'And she lived happily ever after' but it doesn't. Esther's story doesn't end here, this is only the beginning. Her beauty got her this far but there was still a long journey ahead. Could her beauty sustain her? Would her favour with the king last?

Mordecai, who raised Esther, was always concerned about her. Even though he had no access to her he still tried to keep in touch with what was happening in her life. Pacing back and forth at the gates of the palace regularly, he continued to pray for her day in and day out. Little news of Esther escaped the palace gates and even the gossip that he did hear might only have been speculation. Mordecai longed to hear from her, to know if she was safe and happy.

One of those days as Mordecai sat at the gates, he overheard two doorkeepers become furious about something. He moved a little closer to hear what the commotion was about only to discover that they were devising a plot to kill the king. Mordecai sent a message to Esther and told her what he had overheard, urging Esther to

Esther's Story

warn the king. The assassination plot was found out and the assassins hanged at the gallows. As with all important events, this event was written down in the records for the King.

Years passed and little news came in or out of the palace gates. A new ruler, Haman, was appointed by the King. He became a powerful man in the kingdom, Prime Minister of Persia in fact. The king commanded that all his servants who were within the palace gates should bow down and pay homage to Haman. Mordecai however refused to bow down to him. *Then the king's servants who were within the king's gate said to Mordecai, "Why do you transgress the king's command?"*

Now it happened, when they spoke to him daily and he would not listen to them, that they told it to Haman, to see whether Mordecai's words would stand; for Mordecai had told them that he was a Jew. When Haman saw that Mordecai did not bow or pay him homage, Haman was filled with wrath.[10]

Haman desperately desired to lay hands on Mordecai but was advised not to as he was a Jew. This upset Haman even more so he plotted to kill all the Jews in Persia and Media. His thoughts must have been along the lines of *'why take out only one when you can wipe them all out'*. He asked the King

Esther or Delilah?

to authorize a royal decree to completely annihilate the Jews and the King agreed, still completely oblivious to the fact that his beloved wife was a Jew.

When Mordecai learned all that had happened, he tore his clothes and put on sackcloth and ashes, and went out into the midst of the city. He cried out with a loud and bitter cry.[11] Esther's maids and eunuchs came and told her about Mordecai's wailing, and the queen was deeply distressed.

Esther asked her servants to take clothes to Mordecai and to take his sackcloth away from him but he refused. She sent her servants to him again to ask him what the cause of his distress was. Mordecai sent a reply back to Esther telling her of the awful plans that Haman had for the Jewish people. Esther, knowing what her cousin was thinking, then sent a reply back saying; *"All the king's servants and the people of the king's provinces know that any man or woman who goes into the inner court to the king, who has not been called, he has but one law: put all to death, except the one to whom the king holds out the golden sceptre, that he may live. Yet I myself have not been called to go in to the king these thirty days."*

So they told Mordecai Esther's words[12].

Esther's attempts to explain to Mordecai that there was nothing she could do fell on deaf ears. Her explanation that

Esther's Story

the king hadn't invited her to see him for quite some time also went ignored. Finally, her appeal to Mordecai for her life, explaining that if she approached the king uninvited he might put her to death, was also ignored. Mordecai only seemed to be interested in the fact that if she visited the king, there was a small chance that he would hold out his sceptre to her. This action would allow her to approach him and not be put to death. Mordecai was adamant despite the obvious great risk!

Esther felt helpless and told Mordecai that she couldn't do anything to help him and the Jewish people. Again, not listening to her reasoning, Mordecai responded saying; *"Do not think in your heart that you will escape in the king's palace any more than all the other Jews. For if you remain completely silent at this time, relief and deliverance will arise for the Jews from another place, but you and your father's house will perish. Yet who knows whether you have come to the kingdom for such a time as this?"*[13]

Esther realised that Mordecai was adamant. She knew that if she didn't do something then God would send someone else to save the Jews but she and her family would die in the process. Mordecai's challenge to Esther reached her heart. She became aware that perhaps God had put her on the throne as queen for this very reason and for this

Esther or Delilah?

precise time. The penny dropped. A decision was made. Esther's life was at risk. She was going to take the risk that would change history but could also result in her death, an outcome that she did not know for sure but a risk she was now willing to take.

Esther sent a message to Mordecai saying, *"Go, gather all the Jews who are present in Shushan, and fast for me; neither eat nor drink for three days, night or day. My maids and I will fast likewise. And so I will go to the king, which is against the law; and if I perish, I perish!"*

Now it happened on the third day that Esther put on her royal robes and stood in the inner court of the king's palace, across from the king's house, while the king sat on his royal throne in the royal house, facing the entrance of the house.

It was so silent you could hear a pin drop! Officials standing around gasped when they saw the queen boldly walking up to the king. Others immediately scrambled to leave and tell their friends of what was happening in the palace. While all this was taking place the king sat with his head down tending to royal business, unaware of the scene unfolding before him.

Esther stood quietly.

What was only minutes seemed like hours.

She waited with baited breath.

Esther's Story

She waited for the king to raise his eyes to her and realise that she was standing before him, uninvited.

The king looked up from his scrolls.

Noticing Esther standing quietly at the end of the court, he smiled, showing his favour toward her, and without hesitation held out *to Esther the golden sceptre that was in his hand. Then Esther went near and touched the top of the sceptre. And the king said to her, "What do you wish, Queen Esther? What is your request? It shall be given to you—up to half the kingdom!"*

So Esther answered, "If it pleases the king, let the king and Haman come today to the banquet that I have prepared for him."[14]

It was a simple dinner invitation.

Esther could have died that day, just because she wanted to invite her husband and his colleague to dinner. But she didn't and that evening she prepared a lovely dinner for the king and Haman. The king's heart was melted and he asked her what she wanted again. Again, he offered her up to half his kingdom. Esther's only request was that he and Haman came back again the following night for another dinner party. Esther continued to win favour with the King as she wooed his heart, fed his stomach and reminded him how much he loved her.

 Esther or Delilah?

In the meantime, the plot thickens. Haman, still angry at Mordecai for continuing to refuse to bow to him, grew restless. Although he was annoyed with Mordecai, his heart was merry because he had been invited to the queen's banquet two nights in a row. He jovially said to his family, *"Besides, Queen Esther invited no one but me to come in with the king to the banquet that she prepared; and tomorrow I am again invited by her, along with the king. Yet all this avails me nothing, so long as I see Mordecai the Jew sitting at the king's gate."*

Then his wife Zeresh and all his friends said to him, *"Let a gallows be made, fifty cubits high, and in the morning suggest to the king that Mordecai be hanged on it; then go merrily with the king to the banquet."*

And the thing pleased Haman; so he had the gallows made.[15] Haman fell asleep that night with a smile on his face, contemplating Mordecai's end and still merry from the queen's dinner. Little did he know that while he was drifting off into a deep slumber, the king was having trouble sleeping.

In the early hours of the morning the king sent for someone to read to him. It so happened that the precise scroll that was chosen to make the king sleepy was the story of what Mordecai had done to save him. The king was reminded through this reading about the assassination plot

Esther's Story

that was planned for him. Suddenly the king sat up in bed and *said, "What honour or dignity has been bestowed on Mordecai for this?"*

And the king's servants who attended him said, "Nothing has been done for him."

So the king said, "Who is in the court?"

Morning had come and *Haman had just entered the outer court of the king's palace* to suggest that the king hang Mordecai on the gallows that he had prepared for him. The king's servants said to him, "Haman is there, standing in the court."

And the king said, "Let him come in." So Haman came in, and the king asked him, "What shall be done for the man whom the king delights to honour?"

Now Haman thought in his heart, "Whom would the king delight to honour more than me?" [16]

Smugly, he thought of what would be best to honour someone, because he was sure the king wanted to honour him. Haman came up with an elaborate ceremony proposal whereby he would be marched all through the city on the king's horse with the king's robes for all the people to see! Little did he know that the king was actually asking how to honour the very man that he wanted to kill, Mordecai.

Esther or Delilah?

Humiliation and rage filled his heart when the king decreed that Haman had to honour Mordecai, the man he intended to hang, in front of the whole city. *Afterwards, Haman hurried to his house, mourning and with his head covered. When Haman told his wife Zeresh and all his friends everything that had happened to him, his wise men and his wife Zeresh said to him, "If Mordecai, before whom you have begun to fall, is of Jewish descent, you will not prevail against him but will surely fall before him."*

While they were still talking with him, the king's eunuchs came, and hastened to bring Haman to the banquet which Esther had prepared.[17]

Haman was obliged to enjoy yet another banquet with Esther and the king. On this occasion he was preoccupied with his own humiliation and even the honour of the queen's banquet could not soothe his raging heart. Reluctantly, he attended the dinner party and when they had enjoyed themselves, the king asked Esther what her request from him was. It was then that Esther decided to tell the king of Haman's plan to kill all the Jews. She also used this moment to reveal to the king that she was a Jew too which meant that she too would be put to death under Haman's order. Esther told the king that she, the love of his life, was going to be put to death by his very own prime minister.

Esther's Story

Then the king arose in his wrath from the banquet of wine and went into the palace garden; but Haman stood before Queen Esther, pleading for his life, for he saw that evil was determined against him by the king. When the king returned from the palace garden to the place of the banquet of wine, Haman had fallen across the couch where Esther was. Then the king said, "Will he also assault the queen while I am in the house?" As the word left the king's mouth, they covered Haman's face. Now Harbonah, one of the eunuchs, said to the king, "Look! The gallows, fifty cubits high, which Haman made for Mordecai, who spoke good on the king's behalf, is standing at the house of Haman."

Then the king said, "Hang him on it!" So they hanged Haman on the gallows that he had prepared for Mordecai. Then the king's wrath subsided.[18]

On that day King Ahasuerus gave Queen Esther the house of Haman, the enemy of the Jews. And Mordecai came before the king, for Esther had told how he was related to her. So the king took off his signet ring, which he had taken from Haman, and gave it to Mordecai; and Esther appointed Mordecai over the house of Haman.[19]

This story ends with the Jews surviving, Mordecai being made the Prime Minister and Queen Esther living the rest of her days with the love and adoration of her husband and

 **Esther or Delilah?**

king. From that time until today, the Jews celebrate The Feast of Purim, which marks the time when the Jews were saved from total annihilation. Queen Esther lived happily ever after with her king in her beautiful castle.

Yes, it sounds like a fairy tale - but it really did happen!

Delilah's Story

Delilah's Story

Sampson was an incredibly strong man, his strength was a gift from God which came with a very specific instruction. From the day he was born until the day he died, God said that he was not to cut his hair. Samson's mother did as God said and did not cut his hair. Samson enjoyed great strength all through his childhood and teens, having never cut his hair. However, Samson grew up and along with his mighty strength, he also developed a weakness. Like most men, he liked beautiful women! After all, who can resist a beautiful woman?

The love of Samson's life was a beautiful woman, Delilah. Sadly, this beautiful woman, like many beautiful women

Esther or Delilah?

today, was not good for him. Delilah was being paid by the Philistines to seduce Samson in order to find out what made him so very strong. The Philistines said to her, *"Entice him, and find out where his great strength lies, and by what means we may overpower him, that we may bind him to afflict him; and every one of us will give you eleven hundred pieces of silver."*[20]

So Delilah, using all of her charm and beauty, said to Samson, "Please tell me what makes you strong. I really, really want to know. Tell me too what would cause you to lose your strength."

Delilah batted her eye lids, pouted her lips and used her voluptuous body to seduce Samson into telling her what she needed to know. As she sat giving him her sexiest smile he said to her, "If you tie me up with seven fresh bowstrings, not yet dried, then I will become weak, and have the usual strength like any other man."

Delilah left Samson while he was having a nap and raced off to tell the leaders of the Philistines what she had discovered. Immediately they set to work and got seven fresh bowstrings, not yet dried, gave them to Delilah and she tied him up with them. Some of the Philistine men came into the room with her, ready to capture Samson when they were

Delilah's Story

sure he was weakened. *She said to him, "The Philistines are upon you, Samson!"*

But he broke the bowstrings as a strand of yarn breaks when it touches fire. So the secret of his strength was not known.[21]

Samson seemed oblivious to what Delilah was up to and so this game continued as she asked him where he got his strength from and he responded with something that was not true. When Samson fell asleep Delilah would try what Samson had told her, the Philistines would come to get him and he would escape.

Delilah became upset and said to Samson, *"How can you say, 'I love you,' when your heart is not with me? You have mocked me these three times, and have not told me where your great strength lies."*

She continued to use the 'if you love me' line on Samson day in and day out. Pestering him daily with her words, she wore him down until he could take it no more. She nagged and nagged and nagged. Samson's soul became vexed to death and he gave in to her. He told her everything about himself and *said to her, "No razor has ever come upon my head, for I have been a Nazirite to God from my mother's womb. If I am shaven, then my strength will leave me, and I shall become weak, and be like any other man."*[22]

 ## Esther or Delilah?

Once again, Delilah lulled him to sleep on her knees. As soon as he had drifted off she called over a man and had him shave off the seven locks of his head. Delilah immediately began to shout and call out to Samson so that he would wake up and as he woke his strength left him. She continued to taunt him saying, "The Philistines are upon you, Samson!"

Samson, being accustomed to Delilah's games, awoke from his sleep and thought that he could shake the Philistines off as before but he could not. Not this time! God had left. God was not with him anymore and when God left so did Samson's great strength.

Shock, horror and utter disbelief filled Samson when he realised what had happened. Before he even had time to collect his thoughts excruciating pain writhed throughout his entire body as they gauged out his eyes. Blood mixed with sweat dripped down his face but no mercy was given as they forced him to walk down to Gaze. He was bound with bronze fetters by the Philistines and taken captive. Within a few short hours, Samson had gone from being the world's strongest man to a mere prisoner slave. As he ground away each day in the prison mill, he recalled how he once had it all. He had the looks, the life and the girl. Most importantly, he had God with him.

Delilah's Story

Samson lived in utter humiliation as a slave and a prisoner. The shackles were holding his body but regret and guilt had taken control of his soul. This once mighty man was reduced to nothing – the joke of the Philistines. He gave up his strength for a beautiful woman but ended up losing both his strength and the woman he loved. His life was wasted and he had nothing to live for.

One evening, while Samson sat bound with his chains of regret as well as chains of steel, the Philistines called upon Samson to perform for them. Their hearts were particularly merry that evening and they must have thought it fun to watch this prisoner perform for them.

Samson was brought down from the prison and placed between two pillars. Of course, having no eyes made him feel insecure and so he s*aid to the lad who held him by the hand, "Let me feel the pillars which support the temple, so that I can lean on them."*

Now the temple was full of men and women. All the lords of the Philistines were there—about three thousand men and women on the roof watching while Samson performed. Then Samson called to the LORD, saying, "O Lord GOD, remember me, I pray! Strengthen me, I pray, just this once, O God, that I may with one blow take vengeance on the Philistines for my two eyes!"

 Esther or Delilah?

And Samson took hold of the two middle pillars which supported the temple, and he braced himself against them, one on his right and the other on his left. Then Samson said, "Let me die with the Philistines!"

And he pushed with all his might, and the temple fell on the lords and all the people who were in it. *So the dead that he killed at his death were more than he had killed in his life.*[23]

Esther or Delilah?

Esther or Delilah?

So girls, which woman are you? Are you an Esther or a Delilah? What do you use your beauty for? Do you use your beauty to help and save, to build up your man, to enable your man to make wise decisions? Or are you a Delilah, do you nag constantly and complain repeatedly until your poor husband can take it no more and he is pestered to the extent that his soul is vexed to death? If you are a Delilah, I can tell you now that your man is living as Samson did - in chains as a joke. He might even feel like he wants to use the last of his strength to kill himself! I am not joking. This is a serious matter and far more common than we care to admit. A man who has no strength has nothing and the thought of death is a comfort to him.

Esther or Delilah?

Samson didn't reach his full potential because he **gave** his strength to a woman. Instead of standing up to her or in this case fleeing from her, he gave in to her. Men, even though your woman might drive you insane as she tries to get her own way, don't give in. Deep down inside she doesn't want to have her own way, she is just testing your strength because she needs to know that you are capable of being strong for her.

If you are married to a Delilah you can't leave her but you can stop her from taking your power! A strong woman can only operate where there is a weak or passive man. If your woman is taking your strength from you it is because you are letting her. Stop allowing it men. You are not designed to be a wimp, you are not designed to be weak and you are not designed to be passive. You are a warrior so start acting like one! If you allow your woman to act like a Delilah you are robbing her. She has the potential to become an Esther if you will rise up and be strong and courageous. It will feel weird at first, you might even feel like you are being mean, but as long as you are not being mean and are only being strong, you are on the right path.

Esther or Delilah?

Can I tell you men a little secret? Women don't want to have their own way all the time. And another little secret, you can never be the only source of a woman's happiness. You could spend your entire life trying to please her, you can exhaust yourself trying to make her happy, only to find out at the end of your life that it was a mission impossible. You weren't designed to keep her happy, you were designed to be strong for her, which may at times mean not giving her exactly what she wants.

If you carefully consider your woman's request and make a decision to give her what she wants because you feel it is right – great! BUT if she pesters you and nags you and you give in to her against your better judgement then you are giving away your strength. Both you and she will suffer if you give away your strength and in the end, you could even lose the woman you love. Fight for her and show yourself the strong man that you are. Don't cross the line and be mean and nasty, just stay firm and sure to be strong.

I was mowing the lawn one day and meditating on this very book, realising that I had the potential right at that very moment to be either an Esther or a Delilah to my husband, to my children and to the men in my church. At once I prayed to God and asked him to please help me to be an Esther to

Esther or Delilah?

my people! As I said the phrase 'my people' I chuckled thinking that I was no queen, who am I to say 'my people' like that! But I knew my heart, it was not an arrogant prayer but it was a sincere prayer and I sincerely meant 'my people' as I understood my role in many people's lives.

Perhaps you could also consider praying this prayer for your people. Yes, you have people too. People that look up to you, people that rely on you, people that you influence. You are always influencing people whether you like it or not, the key is to be a good influence and not a bad one.

So who are your people? Perhaps you are at school and your school is your 'kingdom', the place where you can carry the saving love of Jesus to all the people. Perhaps you are a stay at home mum and don't consider yourself to be ruler of much. I tell you the power of one woman in a family is enough to change an entire nation, be an Esther to your husband and children.

It's the same with children, spoilt children are unhappy children. Children that are disciplined in a loving way feel more secure and content in life. No matter how much us women try and convince our man that we want something, our men have to be strong and seek God for wisdom to know what is best. This takes guts, this is what makes a strong man. A man who has the strength to say no to his wife, even

Esther or Delilah?

though it will displease her, is a strong man. Seriously, because he knows what is coming if he doesn't give her what she wants. Perhaps some crying or some nasty words or some manipulation. Any man who can put up with that in order to do what is right is a real man in my eyes. Hopefully, us girls will learn to respect our men's strength and we will minimise our emotional reaction to their leadership. We should admire this quality in a man and not resist it.

EXAMPLE:
Here is an example. My friend in South Africa sent me a letter to raise financial support for her mission work. She is a good friend of mine and immediately I wanted to say yes as soon as I read her letter. I had the reply prepared, it was typed up and awaiting a simple click of the 'send' button. I was ready to commit to supporting her financially on a monthly basis.

I too had sent many letters out over the years requesting financial support and I knew too well how discouraging and how disheartening the steady stream of negative replies was.

I went to Eric to see if he was OK with what I proposed to do before I sent the reply to her. Here follows the proposed letter and Eric's response:

Esther or Delilah?

Hi Anne,

I received your letter in the post today and I want to give you an immediate YES! Yes to whatever you need from me that I can give.

You know, we have tried to raise support as we are unpaid in ministry and the answer has always been NO. I have asked established authors and pastors to read and endorse my books and the answer has always been NO. I have asked people to help spread the word about all our attempts at sharing the gospel through our music and books, the answer is always NO. No because they have no time and no money. I am so fed up of the word NO.

So to you my friend, I come against these awful NO's and I say YES! Yes I have time to pray for you, yes I have time to help and yes I have money to share with you. Whatever I can do to serve you and this awesome ministry - I will. If we don't have time and money to help each other then we will get nowhere in this life!

I Love you my friend, I am proud of the woman you have become!

Love Angela xxx

Esther or Delilah?

Immediately Eric said no. His very firm response was that we had to support our own family and were not in a position at that point in our life to make a monthly commitment. However, he went on to say that we could send her a once off gift of money when we had some available.

I went nuts at Eric, well on the inside anyway. On the outside I calmly but tearfully told him how important it was to me. I told him how these were seeds that we could sow and that we would reap a harvest. I even used Bible verses to show him the error of his way. Eventually, I resorted to telling him how stingy he was and how it was not fair that I had to be stingy too just because he was.

After trying to convince him in every possible way and after getting really angry with him, I mean really angry, I went to God to tell on him. I was seriously so angry that my husband wasn't a generous, giving man.

So I took my dilemma to God!

I said, "God, I want to give, I want to be free to give whenever I want. I trust my husband's judgement but on this occasion he didn't judge anything as he never even bothered to hear my heart. God please show me what to do and how to respond to Anne."

Instantly heaven spoke! I was quickly reminded of these two verses:

Esther or Delilah?

Matthew 10:8

Heal the sick, cleanse the lepers, raise the dead, cast out demons. Freely you have received, **freely give.**

Acts 3:6

Then Peter said, "Silver and gold I do not have, **but what I do have I give you**: In the name of Jesus Christ of Nazareth, rise up and walk."

As I sought answers from God I remembered these two Bible verses. The first verse, Matthew 10:8, spoke of giving freely as I have received. I understood this and wanted to give freely as I had received. I noticed that none of this giving was financial. Hmm, interesting, but I still don't understand God.

The next verse that popped to mind was Acts 3:6 which spoke of giving what I had to give and not trying to give what I didn't have.

"OK God, I get this concept too, but I still don't understand what you are trying to say? Are you saying that I should not give financially? But I want to be generous with finances, I want to sow financially."

"Angela, give what you can, not what you can't. I see your heart but if Eric says you can't give then you simply aren't

Esther or Delilah?

able to give. Give what you are free to give. I will show you the way. I will make you free to give."

So I pondered on this situation and on what I believed God was showing me. In this situation what was I free to give? Eric had said that I could give a once off gift of financial support to Anne, but not the monthly support that I desperately wanted to give her. That was step one – the most obvious one – a once off financial gift. Next, I was free to give her my prayer support. Although this seemed second best to me it was probably the most important thing.

If I were to go all the way and genuinely intercede for her and her ministry, I would be giving her a far greater gift than cash. Just like the disciples gave the crippled man a far greater gift too, they gave him the ability to walk rather than a few coins. What the disciples gave changed his life, it redefined his future, which is much more than a few coins would have done.

Now, looking back about six months, I realise that he was right – one hundred percent, absolutely right. Not only was he looking out for his family but he was also using his God given wisdom and discernment. He is generous in so many ways and had this been the right thing to do I am sure he would have agreed to give. I have no doubt that any form of stinginess was his motivation as we share everything we have

Esther or Delilah?

with whomever we can, we give our money to our church and we give up so much for other people. Eric was protecting his family, the Bible clearly says that he who can't provide for his own family is worse than an unbeliever.

What Eric did took strength. He knew what was right, he was unemotional about it and he didn't buckle under the pressure, under the attack, under the nagging from his wife. He stood strong and firm and confident in his decision. Today, I respect him so much more because of that day and others like it. He showed no Samson qualities at all. He didn't buckle under pressure from me. He didn't give up and give in. God didn't leave him and take his strength away either. Too often men give up, give in and buckle under the pressure of a nagging wife, but what they don't realise is that they might just be losing a lot more than a battle with their wife.

Who knows what else they may be losing? Wives, we must not put our husbands in such a position. Samson lost so much; he lost his life, his potential, his God given destiny and everything else only to be a slave. Why? Because he gave into the nagging of a woman! How badly do you want your own way women, enough to kill your husband? You may not physically kill him, you might just kill his hopes, dreams and his ability to lead an abundant life. On the other hand, you

Esther or Delilah?

might actually send him to an early grave as your nagging could easily cause him serious health problems.

I am learning that I can truly trust my husband as he is a wise man who is strong for me. I would have regretted making yet another financial commitment that we couldn't cope with. I would have felt the weight of it for a long time and would have resented my husband for not protecting me from an emotional decision. But I don't resent him. I deeply respect him so much more than ever before. In fact, I was so relieved that he was able to stand up to me. As you witnessed, I put up quite a terrible fight about the whole thing. It was not pretty. Admitting it to you makes me cringe and I still feel ashamed for trying to manipulate Eric's wise decision.

You can learn a lot from my mistakes and together we can all learn from the mistakes and successes of the women in the Bible. They too responded either very well to their husband's guidance or their response was extremely poor. Either way, their response to their husband determined a particular outcome.

Let's take a look at some fascinating comparisons between Esther, Vashti, Zeresh and Delilah :

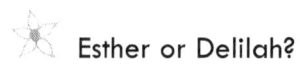 Esther or Delilah?

Esther's Qualities

Took responsibility
Undemanding
Patient
Submissive

Vashti's Qualities

Ignores responsibility
Stubborn
Rebellious
Disobedient

Esther's Attitude to Men

Respect

She empowered the men in her life by showing respect. (Mordecai, Haggai and her husband)

Vashti's Attitude to Men

Humiliation

She humiliated the men in her life

Esther's Attitude to Life

Lived for a purpose

Vashti's Attitude to Life

Lived for herself

Esther's Outcome

Saved her nation

Vashti's Outcome

Lost everything

Esther or Delilah?

Zeresh's Qualities	Delilah's Qualities
No responsibility	No responsibility
Inpatient	Manipulated
Foolish	Nagged
Quick to speak	Pestered

Zeresh's Attitude to Men	Delilah's Attitude to Men
No Respect	No Respect
Her attitude played a part in killing her man	She robbed and killed her man

Zeresh's Attitude to Life	Delilah's Attitude to Life
Lived for nothing	Lived for money and material things and would do anything to get what she wanted

Zeresh's Outcome	Delilah's Outcome
Lost everything	Destroyed her people and the Godly potential of the man she claimed to love

Esther or Delilah?

Esther

Esther was a woman who knew how to treat men and she chose to treat them in the way that she knew to be right. Even when she wasn't treated fairly by being taken prisoner, she still treated all the men in her life with respect. The result was that she had the love and admiration of her husband and the respect of the people she led.

Throughout her story you read of how she had won their favour. The result was incredible! An entire nation was saved. Do you have favour with the men in your world? Have you considered what sort of impact you could be having in so many lives as a result of such a simple thing like how you treat men? Perhaps you were hurt by a man or abused by a man. I know that you think all men are the same deep down inside and one day they will only hurt you again. So you keep your defences up.

Let it go.

By treating men with respect, you are not letting them off the hook for all the bad things that have happened to you. You are not saying that it's OK to be hurt and mistreated. By treating men with respect you are unleashing your potential to be an Esther. If you struggle with men, do it for God, do it for yourself and see how your world will change.

Esther or Delilah?

Vashti

Vashti was a woman from a privileged background who should have had manners and understood her role as queen. It was clear from her response to her king that she did not respect him and his wishes. We can also see from her response that she did not consider the influence that she had on the women that she was leading. The result was that she lost everything.

Zeresh

Not much is said about Zeresh but it is clear that she was just one of the crowd in many ways, as in the three times she was mentioned, it always mentioned Haman's wife and friends. Nothing about her stood out, she didn't seem to stand for anything or live for anything. When her moment came to shine she gave foolish, quick tongued advice which cost her husband his life and caused her to lose her home.

Delilah

Delilah was a beautiful woman just like Esther and she used her beauty just like Esther too. However, her motives were impure and her methods were distasteful. All she wanted was money and so she used a wonderful Godly man to get what she wanted without considering her people or God.

 Esther or Delilah?

You

What about you? If you were to draw a chart of yourself, what would it look like? Determine your own outcome in this life. Take a long, hard and honest look at who you are, write down who you really see yourself to be NOW and then write down who you want to be in your FUTURE.

Don't accept things as they are, you still have time to rewrite your future. Write your own fairy tale life, determine your own history. You have the power of choice, you are not a victim of this life, so be honest with yourself and write out your plan for your future.

Your Qualities

NOW	FUTURE

Esther or Delilah?

Your Attitude to Men

NOW	FUTURE

Your Attitude to Life

NOW	FUTURE

Your Outcome

NOW	FUTURE

Esther or Delilah?

Men, ask God for wisdom and trust what God gives you. Your woman wants a strong man, she won't respect a wimp, she will grow to resent you, perhaps even hate you in the years ahead. You might have to suffer a bit of nagging or abuse at first but if you want to build a relationship that lasts and if you want true respect from your woman, you have to give her what is best and not what is easiest. You have to give her what she really needs and don't give her whatever she wants just to keep the peace. Men, be strong, lead your woman no matter what it takes.

Women, be beautiful and trust your man. He will make mistakes as he learns to be strong but cover him with your love. You will only look even more beautiful to him as he sees your grace covering him.

Influence

Influence

*L*eadership carries a high price and a great deal of responsibility. Vashti's rebellion showed her lack of understanding of her influence or perhaps she did understand but didn't care. Either way, she had a responsibility to her people.

For everyone to whom much is given, from him much will be required.[24] Before we desire great position or any sort of influence in this life, we should seriously consider the high price that comes with it. Before leading a church with my husband I thought it looked like a great 'job'. Since being entrusted with the role I have realised that although it is very rewarding, pastoring is probably one of the most difficult things that a person could do! I have cried many times and

Esther or Delilah?

wished I had not agreed to take on this role. It never occurred to me to count the cost and actually take time to understand what the role of a pastor and church planter entails. Since realising the enormity of the role I have counted the cost and committed to the journey. Sadly, many church leaders don't make it, the pressure gets to them and they either fall into sin or they quit and move into secular employment.

All celebrities, whether Christian or not, influence the world around them, many of them don't even realise the importance of their role as a celebrity. Movie stars, singers, pro-athletes, motivational speakers, etc all carry a position of great influence and sadly many of them too fail and cause many young people to go astray.

You don't need to be a celebrity to have influence, no matter what your station is in life, you are influencing someone. If you are a mother you are having a significant influence on your children. No matter what your convictions and behaviour are, you are moulding your children and shaping their perception of what is normal. I am sure my parents never thought this way but the way I grew up created a foundation in my mind for what I perceived as normal. This mindset dramatically affected the way I viewed life, men, career, family and so much more. Since realising

Influence

the dramatic effect my parents had on me, I have come to take my role as mother very seriously.

If you take a look around you at the hurting and broken world, you will see the fruit of lack of parenting. Parents these days think that having a baby is cute and when the cuteness wears off they are pretty much left to navigate their way through the rough waters of life on their own. TV, movies, magazines and friends begin to mould the child and assist them in growing up into yet another dysfunctional adult. This is the norm, a good parent has become the exception! As I observe poor parenting my heart is grieved as it is blatantly obvious that they are only doing a fraction better than their parents did.

Influence can be as seemingly insignificant as parenting or as huge as leading a country. However, no matter how we view these roles, each influential role is as important as the other. As a mother or father, do you know what your child will grow up to be? Perhaps they are the next Bill Clinton or Billy Graham, how do you know? Your influence is setting the foundation that will determine which 'Bill' they will become.

If you take the time to understand the principle of influence you will be more equipped to shape those around you.

Esther or Delilah?

Esther 1:17

For the queen's behaviour will become known to all women, so that they will despise their husbands in their eyes, when they report, 'King Ahasuerus commanded Queen Vashti to be brought in before him, but she did not come.'

Vashti was banished because she didn't understand her influence but the leaders of her nation did. They knew that all women looked up to her and admired her, she was a Queen after all, a highly influential role in any nation. The King was advised that if Vashti was allowed to behave in this manner then her influence would spread throughout the entire region and all women would treat their husbands in the same manner.

All four women that we have looked at used their influence. Esther won the king's favour and used her influence with him to get her own way, which was to save her people.

Vashti had influence over the women of *one hundred and twenty-seven provinces, from India to Ethiopia*[25]. She didn't understand that and seemed to be oblivious to her responsibility with this influence. Perhaps she was aware but didn't care about the consequences. No matter what her thoughts were on this matter, she didn't use her influence

Influence

wisely and this cost her everything. She lost her husband, her home and her position of influence.

Have you ever considered the alternatives? Perhaps Vashti could have submitted to her husband but at the appropriate time requested an audience with him to express her discomfort with being paraded in front of the drunken men. This response could have allowed her to show respect to her husband, set an example of submission but also allowed her to be excused from the activity that embarrassed her. Put yourself in her position and see how many possible alternatives there were to plain rebellion. If Vashti had understood her influence, valued her influence and understood the consequences of her actions, I am certain that she would have done things differently.

Delilah was a woman who had influence too. She was obviously a very physically attractive woman which automatically got her the attention of men. This influence could have been used for so many different purposes. Esther might have been equally attractive but we can see how these two beautiful women used their influence in very different ways. Delilah chose to sell herself short. She accepted a short term benefit for long term consequences. Delilah chose money over character and sacrificed what

Esther or Delilah?

could have been perhaps an amazing relationship with a wonderful man for this short term gratification.

Delilah's influence was over a man. This position is a position that many of us find ourselves in today. If you are in a relationship and you know that your man really loves you then I can assure you that you have a great deal of influence over him. I have never known a man who really loves a woman who is not influenced by her. A man in love will do almost anything for the women he loves. Samson is a prime example of this, he gave up his strength and his life because of his love for Delilah.

Don't take your influence over your man lightly, you could be influencing him for good and bring out the best in him or could be just like Delilah and ruining him! If you are sure he loves you then I can assure you that you are influencing him for either good or bad. There is nothing in between, you are either lifting him up and helping him be all he can be or you are breaking him down and robbing him of his God given potential.

Delilah was intentionally ruining Samson. Her motivation was clear. She knew what she was doing and she knew how to do it. If you are ruining your man I am sure that you are not as intentional as Delilah. Perhaps you are ruining your man without realising it. You are not a bad woman but

Influence

perhaps you are an ignorant woman. Please consider if you are doing exactly what Delilah did with her influence. Please choose to break free from your ignorant behaviour. Examine yourself[26] and make sure that you are fully aware of your intentions with your man. Are you actively committed to building him up? If not then it is entirely possible that you are intentionally or unintentionally breaking him down.

Haman's wife was another woman who used her influence to kill her husband. As we observed, she was quick to speak and Haman was quick to respond to what she said. This clearly demonstrates that she had influence over her husband. If she had no influence then we would see no record of Haman taking any advice from his wife. That section would simple have been omitted from the Bible because it would have bore no relevance to the story. But it was relevant – highly relevant – because as a result of her influence, Haman wound up dead!

Are you quick to tell your husband your opinion? Do you very quickly lash out at him or do you offer him your opinion without first giving it careful thought? There are many verses in the Bible that advise us to be slow to speak[27], especially the sort that is said in anger[28] but rather to be gentle and quiet[29]. Clearly, Haman's wife was not the quiet and gentle sort but rather the sort of woman that reacts in anger and

Esther or Delilah?

has an opinion about everything under the sun. Carefully examine yourself and judge[30] yourself. Are you a bit like Haman's wife? Do you give your man quick advice, do you express your opinion freely without careful consideration to the consequences of your advice? Is it possible that your advice could cost your husband his job, money, friends, relationship with other family members, position at church or perhaps even his life?

Please don't take this lightly; you have no way of knowing the future and the consequences of your quick tongue. I am quite certain if Haman's wife knew the outcome she would have shut up right from the start.

Esther is our prime example here of what a woman should do with her influence. She was no different than the other women in many ways but what caused her to save her people was her understanding of several important factors, one of them being her influence. She knew that her husband had once been very attracted to her. This gave her confidence that she could win his favour again when she needed it to influence his decision. Self control was displayed and a tamed tongue in a time of great tension, something that few of us can own to. She didn't barge in and cry at the King's feet and demand that he did something, a response that most of us would have and something that

Influence

most of us would justify doing. She didn't use a high pitched whiney squeak when she expressed her disstress to her husband either.

Esther understood that she had influence but she sought God first. She kept calm and took her time to come up with a good strategy so that her influence would produce the best possible result. We will take a look at the other qualities she used in the pages to come, but with regards to her influence, she used it wisely, with restraint and extreme beauty. Can you say that you do the same? I know I would struggle to admit to it but I am inspired by Esther to become that sort of woman - a woman who knows how to use her influence.

Respect

Respect

Respect and trust are close friends. Esther demonstrated a great deal of respect to Mordecai which in turn cultivated a trusting relationship. Esther showed respect to Mordecai by trusting him and acting upon his advice. The respect given caused Mordecai to feel loyal to Esther even though he didn't need to continue worrying about her as he did. Even though she was under new authority she still showed him respect and considered what he said to her. She did not have to do this and would not have been wrong if she did not do as he said, but she wanted to as she genuinely trusted him.

Esther or Delilah?

Ephesians 5:33

Nevertheless let each one of you in particular so love his own wife as himself, and let the wife see that she respects her husband.

Respect in the original Greek comes from the word phobeō which as you know is what we know in English as phobia. Phobeō means to frighten, to be alarmed; by analogy to be in awe of, that is, revere, be afraid, exceedingly fearful or to have reverence.

As wives we are meant to respect our husbands in this way but I have never met a twenty first century woman who has this sort of respect for a man. We resist such reverence; we listen to society that tells us that this is not what God meant in the Bible. I too believed this for a time but deep down inside I can see the beauty of showing respect to people and more specifically to my husband.

Esther demonstrated this sort of respect and trust to every man in authority over her. At first she demonstrated this to Mordecai, even after she was no longer under his authority and living in the palace. In the palace she showed respect to Haggai, the man who was placed in authority over her to prepare her for the King. Finally she showed respect to the King who became her husband.

Respect

How many men are in authority over you in your life? Do you show respect to them? Have you considered that one thing could lead to another and that the respect you are currently displaying or not displaying could be leading to the next big thing in your life, or not?

Are you waiting for a husband? Are you showing respect to your father? Not just lip service to impress, genuine reverence. Are you respectful to your male colleagues or the men at church? You may not realise this but your future husband could be observing how you treat the men in your world as an indication to what sort of woman you are. He might see that you do not show respect and will steer clear of you or hopefully he sees how much you do show respect. A man looking for a wife will definitely be looking for a woman who knows how to show respect, even if it is unconsciously done on his part.

It is a certainty that the way you treat men now will be the way you will treat your husband in the future. Watch yourself, check your attitude. If you see you do have a problem with respect deal with it right away, don't wait until you are married. You will attract who you are. You will attract the sort of person that you are. If you are rude and disrespectful then it is likely that you will attract a rude and disrespectful person. The best thing you can do is start

Esther or Delilah?

working on your attitude to men so that you can attract a man who has a good attitude towards women.

Do you have a husband but are yearning for a promotion at work? How do you treat your husband? How do you treat your colleagues? There are countless scenarios where you could be holding yourself back from your destiny because of your lack of respect for men. I am not pointing the finger in any way here, I too am on a journey to learn how to best respect the men in my world. Women who know how to respect men at work will find favour when the women who have no respect will not.

If you truly want to advance your career make sure you are treating the men in your workplace with respect. Be kind, polite and decent not only to your superiors but even those who work in an inferior position to you. Respect every man in your workplace from the janitor to the director. Do this to honour God. Do this to show others how it is done. Be an inspiration to other women too. Lead the way in this area, giving them permission to behave like a lady.

Most of my life I have been arrogant and proud. The truth is that I was extremely insecure in who I was which caused me to act this way. You will find most people who seem arrogant are actually extremely insecure and unsure of themselves. My deep insecurity caused me to treat people

Respect

as inferior to me. If I managed to push them down then I would be lifted up by default and would of course feel better about myself. Too often I would show my superior knowledge on a subject or my skill in a certain area to gain acceptance from my peers. Insecurity was the root cause of this arrogance but the fruit was lack of respect to others.

Looking back I cringe at the person I was. Slowly, as I have dealt with insecurity I have managed to humble myself in order to lift people up rather than the other way around. In past times I would even see all my husband's faults, especially in areas that I excelled at and would think less of him as a result. Respect was one thing that I was unable to show any man in my life. My past had taught me that all men were the same and that if I didn't keep them at a distance they would hurt me. My safety net was the distance I kept between a man and my heart. I did not and would not fear a man!

My past had made me tough and my perception of men was that they could not be trusted. Before I could ever respect a man I had to learn to trust. This has perhaps been one of the most difficult lessons of my life. My mind and heart had to be completely rearranged in order to even begin to understand trust let alone offer it. Perhaps Esther was raised well. Surely she was taught well by her parents and

Esther or Delilah?

Mordecai. She definitely had not been badly hurt or abused by a man it seems. Trust and respect probably came naturally and quite easily for her. It was in her nature to be that way because she had not been damaged and did not have a reason to be any other way.

But what about the rest of us?

Many of us have a very different upbringing to Esther. Too many of us have been damaged by a man in some way. Although this is not an excuse for poor behaviour it is a very real issue in many women's lives. I want to address this so that you don't feel bad because you don't show respect as Esther did. Yes, Esther had the right attitude but no, she probably didn't have all the baggage that you and I have. And so, with this in mind, please don't feel terrible if you sincerely struggle with respecting men. You are not a bad person because you have this struggle, you are simply a bruised person.

God knows.

He understands.

Jesus says, *"He who is without sin among you, let him throw a stone at her first."*[31]

In the same way I am sure Jesus would say to you, let no one judge you and *"neither do I condemn you; go and sin no more"*[32] In other words, now that you recognise that you

Respect

have not been treating men well, change the way you treat them. Ask God for forgiveness. Ask Him to help you be free from the hurt and resentment that has caused you to feel the way you do. Ask God to help you forgive the men that have hurt and suppressed you. Ask God to help you treat men in a way that would please Him.

Now, quite a few years on, I can see how important trust is in order to cultivate healthy respect. Fear is an element of respect but not the only part of respect. In Esther's case this fear was very real as she could have lost her life when she had to approach her husband.

M2M Men, you can't force a woman to respect you. If she fears you because of your domination you might have a form of respect but I don't believe it is the respect that God intended. Loving your wife as Christ loved the Church and died for her, as it says in Ephesians 5:25, is the key to encouraging your wife to respect you. Also in Ephesians 5:33 it says that each one of you in particular should love his own wife as himself. Did you notice that this verse came before the part that mentioned that wives should respect their husband?

Esther or Delilah?

You cannot demand respect, no matter how much you need it. It is her choice to be a Godly woman who respects her husband or not. What you can do to help her make wise choices, is to love her and help her be the Godly woman that deep down inside she longs to be.

Love her as you love yourself; give her the level of love that equals the level of respect that you desire.

Submission

Submission

Submission is one of the most misunderstood words of our time. Yet, the power within the act of submission, when fully understood, is incredible. I have wrestled with God about this word! Not because I don't want to submit or because I do find it hard to submit but because I didn't fully understand what it meant to submit. Does submission mean that am to be an automated robot and do exactly as my husband says? No, I don't think so. Does submission mean that I should do everything that my husband says even though I have a different opinion? Perhaps, but I still don't think so. So what exactly is submission?

 Esther or Delilah?

Did it ever cross your mind that Jesus, while He was here on earth, was the perfect example of how to be a great wife?

Yes I know Jesus was a man!

1 Corinthians 11:3
But I want you to know that the head of every man is Christ, the head of woman is man, and the head of Christ is God.

Did you see it? No? Let me show you...

"The head of Christ is God."

Herein lies our key, if we watch how Jesus was towards God then we have our perfect example. Jesus was in perfect submission to God as His head. If we want to be all we can be as women then it would be good to study Jesus' attitude towards God. The principle is not that of a father towards a son or a wife towards a husband, what we are looking out for is the attitude of submission.

Taking Esther as an example of perfect submission, I see a woman who understood that her husband had the final say, but needed him to say something specific in order to save her people. Did she manipulate him then? No, I can't see that

Submission

God would have blessed that. So there has to be a fine line between manipulation and submission then, don't you think? Is submission accepting what your husband says as the final word on something, perhaps?

Manipulation, however, seems to be the art of getting him to change his mind by any means possible, which of course is very wrong. Yes I see Esther doing something very close to the line but yet so perfectly executed. Let us learn from her and see how we can be in submission to our husbands, genuine submission, without stepping over the line into manipulation.

Firstly, Esther submitted to God. Submitting to God first is a great key laden with power and meaning. *Wives, submit to your own husbands, as to the Lord,* is the instruction given to us wives. In order to truly be submissive to our husband we need to start with being submissive to God. Without having this sort of relationship with God, I fear submitting to your husband might be a little tricky. You see, if you cannot submit to the One who is perfect then how will you find the strength to submit to an imperfect man?

Let's take a step back for a second. Submission is a biblical principle for unity and harmony in all human relationships. Instructions are given to various people in the Bible to submit, not only wives. Submission is quite the

Esther or Delilah?

opposite of rebellion, which is the original sin causing the fall of Lucifer and the fall of humankind. Choosing to be submissive is choosing to operate in the opposite spirit to rebellion. If we consider submission then as the opposite spirit to rebellion, we can see more clearly the importance and beauty of having this nature.

Take one step closer to understanding submission by understanding the very nature of submission. Submission is the opposite of rebellion and so we should submit to God, to authority[33], to our husbands[34] and to each other[35] in the body of Christ. Submission and sin are almost antithetical. Perhaps, if we understand the divine order of creation and that submission is not only an instruction to women, then we can begin to embrace the fact that we must submit to our husbands.

Husbands have to submit to authority too and certain authorities in our lives have to submit to the authority in their lives. Birds have to submit to their migration patterns and hedgehogs have to submit to hibernation. It's quite simple when you realise that all of creation is based on the principle of submission. Jesus was our ultimate example in this area, if ever there was a human being that understood submission and chose submission, it was Him.

Submission

Jesus our example

"Father, if it is Your will, take this cup away from Me; nevertheless not My will, but Yours, be done"[36]

These words captured the heart of Jesus' submission to His Father. Jesus had a will of His own, He did not want to suffer and be crucified, He even asked God to take that plan away from Him. In the very same sentence Jesus submitted. It was through Jesus' submission, that the curse brought upon us through Satan's rebellion, was reversed.

Wow, what an example! Do you feel more inspired to be submissive now? I know I do. Jesus is our ultimate example and Esther is a great example too. She also knew that in her submission her life was at risk. The difference between Esther's decision and Jesus' decision was that Jesus knew that in His submission he would definitely die. Esther only knew that there was a possibility that she would die.

What are we complaining about? Is your submission life threatening? Does your submission result in the possibility of death? Perhaps a death to your pride or ego, but certainly not physical pain! Why then, do most of us still resist the word submission? It's a little prick on the finger compared to excruciating pain on the cross. How dare we even compare

Esther or Delilah?

such things? Submission is a necessary part of life and a simple request from God. He asks wives to submit to their husbands. He asks this because He has a very good reason and a very divine order for all of creation. Who are we to question or even rebel again the Almighty God?

I speak so harshly with such passion first at myself. This is not directed at you but I am asking myself these questions. The next time I am faced with a conflict about submitting to my husband I am going to force myself to mentally gaze at Jesus on the cross. Then I will realise the small price I have to pay to keep order in my little world. To be honest, I can now count submitting to my husband as a privilege.

Esther must have known this. She understood the value and power of her submission. As we explore this concept I pray that you too see what God wants to unleash in your life, your family, your church, your school or your workplace. A woman who truly knows how to submit is both fully powerful and completely beautiful.

Esther was such a woman I am sure. She showed her character through her continued submission to the one who raised her, Mordecai, and then to Hegai and finally to her husband and King. Ultimately she showed submission to God first which guided her in her submission to everyone else that she needed to submit to. Submission is not blind obedience;

Submission

it is the simple understanding of roles and acting accordingly, trusting the one that has authority over you.

Lucifer was given one of the highest levels of authority in God's chain of command but yet he was still not satisfied — he wanted to be equal with God.[37] Perhaps those of us who don't want to submit are on par with Lucifer in attitude then. God's ways are higher than our ways[38] and we cannot begin to debate with God about why or why not we should submit. Do not test God, if you behave as Lucifer behaved, looking for equality, then I dare say you might fall as Lucifer fell. He not only lost his position but he also lost everything that God gave him. *For I say to you, that to everyone who has will be given; and from him who does not have, even what he has will be taken away from him.*[39]

It has been said that submission is not blind obedience, and I agree of course, but when it comes to God perhaps it is. I can't understand God and why He made things the way He did but I obey Him anyway. Not because He is forcing me to but because I want to.

My confidence lies in the fact that I know that He knows me better than myself and everything He says and does is for my best interests. So in that area, yes my submission is blind obedience, I totally trust Him and I don't need to know why He asks me to do certain things.

Esther or Delilah?

My husband is in authority over me and so is the government and I should submit to them too but as with my submission to God, it is my choice whether or not I do so.

M2M Men, your wife is free to choose whether or not to submit to you. If your wife is stubborn, rebellious and not submitting to you, she will face the consequences.

Your role as husband is not to force her into submission or punish her as a child if she does not submit; your role remains to love her. *A soft answer turns away wrath, but a harsh word stirs up anger.*[40] If you respond to her rebellion with a soft answer rather than a harsh word, you will win her respect and submission will follow soon enough.

Remember, God loves you too, even on your bad days. God loves you even in your rebellion. Put yourself in her shoes and ask God to show you how you can best love her. She is accountable to God for her submission to you and you are accountable to God for your love to her. Just love her, love never fails[41]. Love is not a feeling that you have for her but a choice that you make. Give her your love by choosing to love her.

Submission

So what is submission then?

Submission is the opposite of pride. It involves humility. Although it is an act of showing weakness it takes a lot of strength to be submissive. It is easy to rise up against someone, to be argumentative and uncontrolled in expressing an opinion.

True humble, obedient submission takes a great deal of self-control and strength of character. A submissive person may take a weaker position but is by no means a weak person. It is a common misconception that submission equals weakness. It is quite the contrary, submission takes great strength of character.

Submission Hierarchy

God
⬇
Husbands
⬇
Wives
⬇
Children

 Esther or Delilah?

This is how most people teach submission – God is over our husbands in authority, God and husbands are over wives, God, husbands and wives are over children.

Another way of looking at it is that children must obey parents and God, wives must obey husbands and God and husbands must obey God.   This is true but only partly. There is so much more to submission that just obeying.

Dictionary = the act of giving something for a
                                 decision to be made by others
Bible   = obedience
Other Ideas =   to yield, to be weak and to
                                 surrender

To yield

Not be **forced** into something or blindly obey but to **choose** to yield causing a **smooth flow** to your life.

Submission

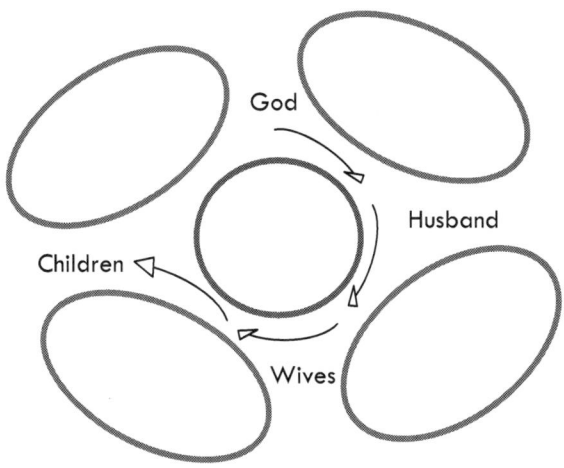

Submission is always a choice – no one can make you submit and you should not force anyone to submit to you. God gave us all free will so who are we to take it away from others?

Imagine driving towards a roundabout and refusing to follow the traffic rule that requires you to yield to the car coming from the right? Is it a traffic suggestion or is it a traffic rule? No matter whether you think it's a suggestion or a rule, not following it will cause a catastrophe.

Isn't this a much nicer way of looking at submission? If you view submission as a traffic circle rather than a hierarchy you might find that it makes more sense to you. Many people resist submission because they feel that if they submit then they are making themselves inferior or less valuable.

Esther or Delilah?

This of course is not what submission means at all. Does considering submission as a traffic circle help you keep your self-worth intact? It made a massive impression on me and clarified so many of my concerns.

It is the same in marriage, you can be in denial about the whole submission thing, but not yielding will most certainly cause quite a mess in your marriage. Someone must yield and God said it should be the woman in a marriage. I don't see you arguing with the police about the traffic rules of a roundabout; doing so would make you look silly! In the same way, stop arguing with your husband about the 'traffic' rules of marriage and just yield.

It's not life threatening, it's simply yielding to allow a good flow to your life. You are the one looking silly when you don't and you are the one causing the 'traffic jam' in your life if you refuse to yield. It all makes sense when you consider an argument as a traffic jam. Clearly you will be able to see that the 'pile up' resulted because no one would follow the 'roundabout rules'. It really does seem silly that we would get into our car and accept traffic rules but ignore the rules for our marriage! Disaster can result from ignoring the traffic rules. In the same way we can expect disaster to result in our marriage if we ignore the principle of submission.

Submission

To be weak

Not to assert yourself **physically** but to **accept** that your strength is less in your **body** both in muscle power and health.

"Husbands, likewise, dwell with them with understanding, giving honour to the wife, as to the weaker vessel, and as being heirs together of the grace of life, that your prayers may not be hindered."[42]

Would you like your husband to honour you? Doesn't that sound wonderful? God does tell husbands to give honour to their wives but there is more to it than that, He says to honour them as the weaker vessel. In fact God actually gives them a little 'threat' by saying that if they don't do this then their prayers will be hindered. I think God was being very serious when He told the men to do this.

If it is so important that men honour us as the weaker vessel why are we going around trying to be strong and in control of everything? Having the honour that God wants our husbands to give us is so beautiful but we need to give up our battle to be so strong and simply be the weaker vessels

 Esther or Delilah?

that we were designed to be. Our men cannot honour us as the weaker vessel if we are not **being** the weaker vessel.

Honour comes from the Greek word timē (pronounced tee-may'), which means to pay a price, a value, that is, money paid, or (concretely and collectively) valuables; by analogy esteem (especially of the highest degree), or the dignity itself: - honour, precious, price, some.

Would you like your husband to treat you like something really precious and valuable? Would you like him to esteem you highly and to honour you? Of course you do, who wouldn't like to be treated like that! The key is of course submission and the specific part of submission is to be weak. If you are the weaker vessel that God make you to be then your husband can give you the honour that God wants him to give you.

Your body was made weaker, you cannot do what a man does as your muscles can't cope and neither can your physical health. God made it that way for a reason, who are we to question Him?

 Men, your wife may not be behaving as the weaker vessel that God made her to be. She is still, however, a

Submission

weaker vessel and should be honoured accordingly, most importantly so that your prayers may not be hindered. She is only wearing herself out by trying to be strong when she was not designed to be this way. Perhaps if you treated her as the weaker vessel, even when she is behaving contrary to that, she might find a clear path to learning to be the weaker vessel God wants her to be.

If you were my husband you would instantly ask for an example after reading this! Here are a few off the top of my head. Weakness can refer to physical weakness, so if you see her doing heavy work, assist her or do it for her. Weakness can also refer to her emotional state. If your wife cries, comfort her and understand that women do need to cry. Don't be annoyed, push her away or tell her to stop crying.

Eve was deceived; she was too weak to resist the devil when he tempted her. Watch over your wife, step in when sales people harass her, and be proactive in helping her resist the devil's temptation. She is weak and the devil's strategy hasn't changed one bit. She needs you to take control and say no when you can see her being deceived. Protect her but don't control her.

The end result will be a more peaceful, beautiful wife with more willingness to submit.

Esther or Delilah?

To surrender

To resist no longer but to give way by letting go and laying down.

How many arguments could you have avoided by simply surrendering? Yes, give in, admit defeat, surrender! You don't always have to be right and even if you are right you don't always have to prove it.

Men want to be the hero, they want a woman to look up to them with wonderment and amazement and see how great they are. Do you really think you are making your husband feel like the hero when you are constantly arguing your point and trying to prove how right you are? What you are in fact doing is bringing him down to size. You are humiliating him so that you can feel better about yourself.

Paul says to "*remind them of these things, charging them before the Lord not to **strive about words to no profit, to the ruin of the hearers**.*"[43] It is also mentioned several times in the Bible that women should be silent in church[44], not argumentative[45] and that her true beauty to God is found in her quiet and gentle spirit[46].

Submission

A very important part of submission is to surrender when necessary and this might involve biting your tongue and keeping quiet – even when you are right and you can prove it with physical evidence!

M2M Men, I have encouraged your woman to submit, surrender, to be weak, to yield to you and to keep quiet when necessary. A tall order but not impossible! When you see her making an effort, please do your utmost to encourage her and support her by saying something lovely to her that will make her feel loved and beautiful. It's probably best not to mention the submission thing if she struggles with it as you might not get the reaction that you would hope for!

At the same time know that your ability to understand her is essential and if you don't try to understand her, your prayers may be hindered. In 1 Peter 3:7, before men are instructed to give honour to their wives as weaker vessels, they are instructed to live with their wives with understanding. Perhaps there is a reason for the order of these things. You might not be able to honour her as the weaker vessel without first understanding her.

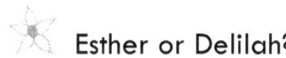 **Esther or Delilah?**

Media has lied to you, women can be understood, do you really think God would have given you an instruction that was not possible to achieve? Be encouraged, He has given the Holy Spirit to you to help you in all things, even this thing. Ask Him to help you understand your wife and as you do, see how your wife, your marriage and your prayer life are all changed.

Everything God did was to bless us; submission is a part of God's divine plan. Imagine if the earth decided not to submit to gravity or the animals decided not to submit to their masters. What if we all decided not to submit to traffic laws or if our children all decided to do exactly what they wanted whenever they pleased?

Surely you can see the necessity of submission in ordinary, everyday life? Being a submissive wife is not different from all the other things in life that need to submit. It is simply a role and a divine order to living. Esther knew how to use her role and her submission to save her nation – imagine what would have happened if she rebelled? Take a moment to consider the other version of the story that could have been written if Esther chose not to submit.

Consider if your life story could be different based on your attitude to submission. How many lives are you influencing each day and consider how your submission or lack thereof

Submission

could be affecting their lives. Esther gained a great deal and lost very little, if anything at all, by choosing to be a submissive woman.

It is quite that simple – give it a try - submit. Submit with a cheerful heart. *So let each one give as he purposes in his heart, not grudgingly or of necessity, for God loves a cheerful giver.*[47]

Submission in the Bible

Considering that submission is not only for women but for many other areas also takes the pressure off. How often do we feel that it's unfair that we have to submit? I believe our response to submission is often due to a lack of understanding of what submission is. Once you take a look at how many other areas of life require submission you will quickly see that submission is intended to order our lives and is not an inferior vs. superior suggestion. I am sure you don't have the same response when you have to submit to the government for example or your leaders in church, or do you?

Take a minute to consider all the areas of our lives that require submission and decide for yourself if you are a submissive person.

 **Esther or Delilah?**

1. **Submit to God -** James 4:7

    Therefore submit to God. Resist the devil and he will flee from you.

2. **Submission to Husbands -** Colossians 3:18

    Wives, submit yourselves unto your own husbands, as it is fit in the Lord.

3. **Submit to Leaders -** Hebrews 13:17

    Obey those who rule over you, and be submissive, for they watch out for your souls, as those who must give account. Let them do so with joy and not with grief, for that would be unprofitable for you.

4. **Submission to Elders -** 1 Peter 5:5a

    Likewise you younger people, submit yourselves to your elders.

5. **Submit to Parents -** 1 Timothy 3:4

    One who rules his own house well, having his children in submission with all reverence.

6. **Submission to Each Other -** 1 Peter 5:5b

    Yes, all of you be submissive to one another and be

Submission

clothed with humility, for "God resists the proud, but gives grace to the humble."

7. **Submit to the Government** - 1 Peter2:13-14

   Therefore submit yourselves to every ordinance of man for the Lord's sake, whether to the king as supreme, or to governors, as to those who are sent by him for the punishment of evildoers and for the praise of those who do good.

8. **Spirits Submit to Believers** - Luke 10:20

Nevertheless do not rejoice in this, that the spirits are subject to you, but rather rejoice because your names are written in heaven.

So if we take our traffic circle of life we can see how important it is that everyone knows whom they should submit to. Without the principle of submission in our lives the world would be in chaos.

There are many other examples of submission cycles in nature. Consider the water cycle for example and how at each stage the water has to submit to the stage 'above' it in order to progress as water. This cycle of evaporation and condensation controls all of the earth's water supply as it evaporates from bodies of water, condenses, precipitates, and returns to those bodies of water. The water cycle is a cycle working in perfect harmony with no arguments as to who does what and who is superior. Just imagine if water was given free will as we were!

Other examples of cycles in nature are metamorphosis, photosynthesis, seedtime and harvest. Can you imagine what would happen if all of creation was given free will as we were? We would end up with cheeky worms that refuse to sleep because they are not tired and leaving the butterfly population to the remote few who know how to submit to their God given order.

Consider if trees decided not to give off oxygen because they couldn't be bothered or were too tired on any given day! What a disaster that would be – we would certainly all die if creation had free will.

Submission is essential to God's order on this planet, it is only us human beings who have determined that we can do whatever we want and then expect no consequences as a result. One day the stones might cry out[48], the mountains and hills will burst into song and the trees may start clapping their hands[49]. When that day comes I wonder what they will have to say about us human beings.

Favour

Favour

Favour is given by God for a reason, it's not only for you to enjoy but for you to use to advance the kingdom.

Esther was already a queen long before a crown was put on her head. I have often heard the saying that a leader is a leader whether she has a title or not. A leader will naturally lead in any situation that requires leadership. Title or recognised status will not change the nature of a true leader.

This is true of Esther too; she had the favour of a queen long before she was officially appointed queen. People looked up to her, admired her and would do anything for her. She ruled them without intending to do so. They looked up

Esther or Delilah?

to her as a leader long before she was given the title. She took responsibility for the people and led them with her graciousness long before she had to do so. This is who she was; she obtained favour wherever she went with all the people that she met.

Have you ever dreamt of being a princess or a queen? It's quite easy to become one, simply start acting like one. Try and develop the character of a princess. Try to love people and lead people no matter what your title or station in life is. You never know what might happen, you never know who you might attract favour from.

Who you are is way more important than what your title is. In fact, a title means very little in reality. A truly beautiful woman has unlimited power at her disposal if she understand her power and knows how to use it. A truly beautiful woman is always growing in Godly character which she values highly, above all else. If *you* want to cultivate this sort of beauty why don't you spend your energy working on your character rather than working hard at climbing the corporate ladder to position or spending hours in front of the mirror and shopping for the latest clothing and accessories? Your character is what will make you stand out and your character will give you favour.

Favour

Attracting Favour

1. Grow in True Humility

James 4:6
God resists the proud, But gives grace to the humble.

A truly humble person is irresistible and they will attract favour from everyone. I have met a few people with this precious quality and somehow they leave you feeling like you want to do whatever they ask or give them whatever they want. They are so unassuming and so pleasant to be around. In Esther 2:15 you will notice that Esther **requested nothing** - she was undemanding and humble in her manners and appearance it seems.

Favour is something that grows, you are not born with it and even Jesus had to grow in favour, which we read about in Luke 2:52, "*And Jesus increased in wisdom and stature, and in favour with God and men*". Jesus even grew in favour with God. He was perfect yet his favour still had to grow. Don't you find this interesting?

Favour from Luke 2:52 comes from the Greek word 'charis' which means graciousness of manner or act, gratitude, pleasure. Jesus was growing in graciousness, gratitude and was pleasant to be around. If Jesus, the son of God, needed to grow in this then surely so should we? Are we gracious, grateful and a pleasure to be around? Or are we harsh, hostile and demanding? True humility is not a natural characteristic; we need to grow into humble women. I believe this is only possible as we grow closer to God and begin to take on His character. It is when we find Him that we find favour from Him too. It says in Proverbs 8:35 that *"For whoever finds me finds life, and obtains favour from the Lord"*.

Isn't that amazing? So not only do we grow in humility as we get closer to Jesus but we also find favour with Jesus. This sort of favour means that we will be acceptable to Him, we will bring Him delight and pleasure. How wonderful is it to know that we bring pleasure to our God? And so, as we grow in humility we will attract favour both from God and from other people.

Now to completely blow your mind, the root word for grace in James 4:6 and for favour Luke 2:52 is exactly the same word, which is the Greek word 'charis'. So when God says He gives grace to the humble He is saying that He gives His favour – the same favour that Jesus grew in. It couldn't be clearer, in order to attract favour we must be humble. If

Favour

we are not humble God will resist us and my guess is, so will other people.

I don't know about you but I find it difficult to be around arrogant people – do you get the picture?

2. Serve with a Sincere Heart

Ephesians 6:7
...doing service, as to the Lord, and not to men

Esther knew who she was serving. No matter whether she was serving Mordecai or Hegai or the King, in her heart she was serving God first and foremost. When you are serving God through everything you do, you will attract favour. You will be irresistible to all whom you serve.

3. Speak Gently

Proverbs 15:1
A soft answer turns away wrath, but a harsh word stirs up anger.

People who speak nicely definitely attract favour! Esther knew how to address a man in a way that made him feel like

Esther or Delilah?

a king. She didn't demand, sulk or throw a tantrum. She probably could have justifiably panicked but she didn't, she kept her cool. Before Esther ever assumed anything or asked for anything, she first said a sentence of beautiful words to her husband, she said, *"If it pleases the king, and if I have found favour in his sight and the thing seems right to the king and I am pleasing in his eyes."*[50]

Esther knew how to speak gently in order to win favour. She used her words beautifully. How many of us take the time to formulate beautiful words when making a request to someone? In fact, how many times have you observed someone speaking nicely when making a request? It is rare these days. I was pleased one day when my five year old son commented on how people in the movies never say please and very seldom say thank you. I was pleased because that made me realise that please and thank you was normal to him and not a foreign concept.

If you want to attract favour, take time to speak nicely and to speak gently. Gentleness can also show humility and respect. Paul instructs Timothy in the Bible that, *opponents must be gently instructed, in the hope that God will grant them repentance leading them to a knowledge of the truth.*[51]

In Proverbs is says that *through patience a ruler can be persuaded, and a gentle tongue can break a bone*[52]. Speaking

Favour

gently will not only give you favour but could be the very thing that causes breakthrough in some very difficult situations.

Timing

Timing

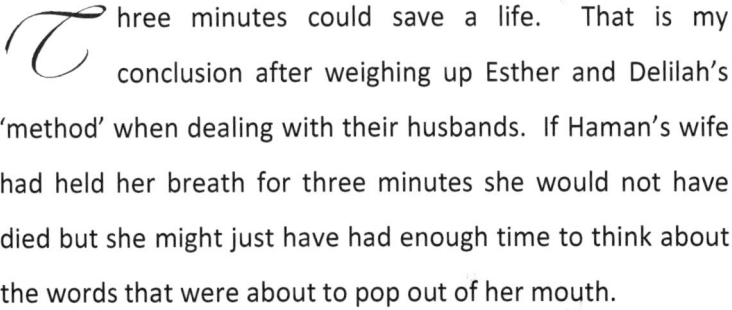

Three minutes could save a life. That is my conclusion after weighing up Esther and Delilah's 'method' when dealing with their husbands. If Haman's wife had held her breath for three minutes she would not have died but she might just have had enough time to think about the words that were about to pop out of her mouth.

Stop reading here for a second, well actually for three minutes, and see how long three minutes actually is! It's a very long time and if you hold your breath much longer than three minutes you surely will die, but on the flip side, if you took just three minutes to think about what you were about to say I can assure you the outcome would be very different. Haman's wife and friends did not take even three minutes to ponder on their advice to him I am sure!

 **Esther or Delilah?**

Esther, however, took a little longer; she also considered life or death timing. She took three days without food or water before approaching her King. If she stayed without water any longer than three days she could have died, so her timing was impeccable. Esther took the perfect amount of time to get God's attention in order to save her people but without harming herself from lack of water. It was perfection. Timing is essential and Esther understood this which is why she didn't rush into anything at all.

First she prepared herself and her 'team' before God – something that Haman's wife did not do. Haman's wife and her 'team' of friends rushed to Haman to give him advice without first consulting God and without even taking a few minutes to think about the possible consequences of their advice.

After Esther's fast she proceeded to the next part of her plan. She did not rush into anything at all, she could have asked the King on the first day when he held out his sceptre to her, but she didn't. She took her time to win his favour before she asked anything. She wooed him with her beauty; she spent time with him to make sure he remembered how much he loved her.

A wise woman will understand the importance of timing and will know how and when to use her beauty! Beauty can

Timing

be unveiled strategically or beauty can be unveiled manipulatively. Both men in the story of Esther are being advised about what to do by their wives, but only one man is offered wisdom.

I am prone to rushing. Since I was a little girl I always heard people telling me to slow down. My school report cards repeatedly said, "Angela is very bright but her work could be a little neater if she didn't rush her work." You would think after several report cards that I would get the message, but no, I continued to rush through life and repeatedly heard the same message at several of my jobs. I also rushed into marriage and definitely didn't consider any timing when having children.

At the same time I have always been complemented on how efficient I am but it does beg the question, am I thorough? Timing is important in everything, only fools rush which is something that I have had to learn the hard way by making a lot of stupid mistakes.

If I Perish, I Perish

If I Perish, I Perish

I am only one,

But still I am one.

I cannot do everything;

but still I can do something;

and because I cannot do everything

I will not refuse to do the something that I can do

Edward Everett Hale

I want to end this section with Esther's words, "If I perish, I perish" because I believe that this will be

 Esther or Delilah?

where we start! If we truly want to be an Esther, a woman of destiny in our time, then we need to be willing to let go of some things. In Esther's case it was her life, she was willing to die for this cause! There are some of you reading this that might need to say the same thing. You might be facing a life and death decision as you consider going into a country at war or a country closed to Christianity. You might have to just do it whilst saying, "If I perish, I perish"

But for most of us I don't believe it is quite that extreme. Most of us are blessed to live in a time where life is relatively easy which makes the death we have to face easier too. Your death might be the death of your finances or of your reputation. You may need to put to death a relationship or a dream that was leading nowhere. There was a time in my life when I had to put to death the business that I really loved. I had sacrificed everything to build my company, D7 Consulting.

Years and a great deal of lost time with my children had passed. Many sleepless nights and large sums of money were a part of the price. I was incredibly passionate about my business and firmly believed with all my heart that it was what I was called to do in order to make money to sow into the kingdom. I wasn't blind to the fact that it took money to build a great church and I wanted to be one of the people

If I Perish, I Perish

that made money to give to my church. You couldn't not fault my faith in this until one day I considered that perhaps it was not what God wanted me to do with my life.

It was a very uncomfortable thought. I had sacrificed so much for my company. My family had supported me all the way and sacrificed a great deal too. My children thought that it would be their inheritance. But the thought lingered and as it lingered I started to see that God was not blessing my work. I had amazing clients that should have turned a huge profit but for some bizarre reason nothing came of it. I had a national team of staff that should have been bringing in more good clients, but not one of them had any success. Rather odd I thought! Not one of them? Something was wrong. I had opportunities to expand internationally but for some reason the people in Malta were dragging their feet. The company seemed perfectly positioned for success and if God wanted to bless my business He most certainly could have – everything was lined up ready for His touch but He didn't touch any of it.

So I prayed and after some uncomfortable incidents with my staff and an honest look at the business bank account, I made the most heart wrenching decision of my life – I gave up my dream. This was the dream that I was willing to die for, this was the dream that I was convinced I was born for;

 **Esther or Delilah?**

this was the dream that I had convinced my friends and family was from God. I was SO absolutely sure that this was what I was meant to do with my life, but for some reason God had not blessed it so I had to let it go.

I grieved.

I felt like a failure. Nothing made any sense any more. I quickly got a job to make up some of the money I had lost so that my husband and children wouldn't be too disappointed in me. I questioned God. I asked Him what was going on. I doubted that I even heard the voice of God as I was sure I had heard Him about the business but clearly I had not as it was no more.

Nothing made any sense.

Time passed and I began to accept the decision I had made. Then God spoke! One night as I tossed and turned He said something that changed my life, "Unless a grain of wheat falls into the ground and dies, it remains alone; but if it dies, it produces much grain." [53]

This made perfect sense to me! My mourning turned to joy, suddenly life made sense again! Yes, my dream had perished but had it? I always knew I was meant to do something big with my life and I thought the company was the 'big thing', but was it? My hope was restored and so was my sense of destiny. I knew that there was still something

If I Perish, I Perish

big in God's plan for my life and allowing the company to perish was all a part of the plan. I needed to allow it to die in order for it to produce much more. And so I began to hope again.

During the season that I worked on my business I also worked on other things. To be more accurate, God was working on His master plan while I was dabbling with my plan. Thankfully He didn't wait for me to stop dabbling before He started His work or else a great deal of time would have been wasted. God was setting me up without me even realising what was going on. God was blessing His plans in my life while I was seeking His blessing on my plans. I laugh now as I write this because I can see how ridiculous it all was!

You see, while I was building my company God was building His church. Every Friday night I would stop my work and open my home to my daughters' friends. Both my girls were in high school and were trying to win their world to Jesus. My husband and I started a youth group to support their efforts and the youth group was growing out of control. Teenagers were getting saved and lives were being changed. It was a beautiful season in our life and God was clearly blessing this area of our life. We quickly realised that we needed to do more for these new converts and the church we attended was an hour's drive away from our home.

Taking them all to church was not viable so we had a meeting with our pastor to ask him for permission to start a discipleship group with them on Sunday afternoons. Our plan was to attend our church in the morning and then take care of our baby Christians in the afternoon.

Well, to cut a long story short, we walked into the pastor's office asking for permission to start a discipleship group and we walked out of his office with permission to plant a church! WHAT? It took a while to sink in but it did eventually 'feel' real when we committed to a launch date. Eric and I had no experience in leading a church, neither of us had ever preached and we most certainly had not anticipated this EVER! Also, neither one of us had ever dreamed of leading a church. The thought had never crossed our mind and we had never, ever planned for this to happen. Nevertheless, we said yes. All this took place during the years that I was building my company. God was working on His dream for us without us even realising it. Perhaps if I hadn't been so distracted with the company I would have freaked out and said 'NO' to this great call from God!

When God reminded me of the verse that speaks of the seed dying and falling to the ground in order to be more fruitful I realised that the death of my business was a very necessary part of His plan for more reasons than I probably

If I Perish, I Perish

even realised. It was essential that I lead a life that counted the cost but still boldly said, "If I perish, I perish".

Can you say the same thing right now?

Think about your life, is God working on His plan in the background because you are too busy trying to make your dream work? Take a step back and have an honest look at your life, is God blessing something without you even realising it? Are you flowing with His blessing or are you fighting what He is blessing because you want Him to bless your own plans? Are you able to say, "If I perish, I perish" and lay down your plans?

It could be that you need to let your reputation perish. Are you a corporate executive and God is calling you to serve the drug addicts and alcoholics in the street? Do you fear what people might say to you at work on Monday when they see you in the street over the weekend hugging a dirty, smelly street person? Are you willing to make a difference no matter what the consequences are to your reputation? Charles R. Swindoll sums it up nicely in his book called Esther when he says about Esther, "She has changed from fear to abandonment and faith, from hesitation to confidence and determination, from concern for her own personal safety to concern for her people's survival. She has reached her own personal hour of decision and has not been found wanting."

Esther or Delilah?

It is time for your own personal hour of decision right now. There is no more time to lose! What needs to perish in your life? Do you need to let go of your reputation? Jesus *made himself nothing, taking the very nature of a servant, being made in human likeness*[54]. If anyone had the right to His reputation is was Jesus, but he let it perish so that He could save us!

Perhaps your finances need to perish, or at least your concept of financial security. Do you have a good savings account, loads of investments and everything nicely under control? Ask Jesus if He needs this money; ask Him what He would have you do with it. Be willing to let it perish for the sake of others. It is good to be a wise steward and good for you if you have managed your money well. I am not suggesting you be unwise but I am suggesting that you ask God if He has blessed your finances for a reason and then be willing to do whatever He asks of you.

Eric and I are currently unpaid pastors, we had to let go of the security of a monthly salary and live off of adhoc income from teaching music. It has been tough, it has been painful at times and it has most certainly been uncomfortable. We had to let our concept of financial security perish so that we could pursue the dream that God has for us. Although on paper, our finances look out of control, I can tell you that we

If I Perish, I Perish

have lacked nothing. And I can assure you that *my God will meet all your needs according to his glorious riches in Christ Jesus*[55] too.

Doing things God's way is SO much more fun than my way! Letting go, losing control, allowing things to perish, is the best adventure I have ever been on and I could not go back to my old ways of having everything figured out and always being in control.

So my question remains, what needs to perish in your life? Is it your dreams for your children? Ouch! Yes I know this one too well too, it's tough when you can see what you think is the best path for your children and then they choose to go down a difference path. But you have to ask yourself if you are trusting in your dreams for them or if you are trusting in God's dreams for them? It's hard to let go – I KNOW! But I trust that if I do, God will have His way in their lives, even though at times it looks like He is not. *And we know that all things work together for good to those who love God, to those who are called according to His purpose.*[56] When it comes to my children I have to believe this and allow my perfect plan for my children to perish so that God's perfect plan can work in their lives.

When Esther said, "If I perish, I perish", she was talking about her actual physical life. She was willing to die. Most of

 **Esther or Delilah?**

us don't have to face such an extreme decision today. Keep it in perspective; you might only have to let one area of your life perish. It's a small price to pay compared to actual DEATH! Rise up woman of God, be all that God wants you to be, and if you perish, you perish!

The Starfish Story

One day a man was walking along the beach when he noticed a boy picking something up and gently throwing it into the ocean. Approaching the boy he asked, "What are you doing?"

The youth replied, "Throwing starfish back into the ocean. The surf is up and the tide is going out. If I don't throw them back, they'll die."

"Son," the man said, "don't you realize there are miles and miles of beach and hundreds of starfish? You can't make a difference!"

After listening politely, the boy bent down, picked up another starfish, and threw it back into the surf.

If I Perish, I Perish

Then, smiling at the man, he said, "I made a difference for that one."

- From the original story 'The Star Thrower' by Loren Eiseley (1907–1977)

You too can make a difference. Yes, you are called to something big but don't sit around waiting for the big opportunity to present itself, get busy making a difference even if it has to be just one starfish at a time, just get busy and then God will get busy working out the big thing in your life, perhaps without you even realising what He is up to – just like He did with me.

Jesus said, *"For whoever desires to save his life will lose it, but whoever loses his life for My sake will save it."*[57] You have nothing to lose, if you perish, you perish and from it you will gain.

A Cause

Esther was willing to perish for a cause. Do you stand up for the cause that presents itself in your everyday life? Often Christians are known for what they are against but not what they are for. In this negative age where Christians are

 Esther or Delilah?

avoided because of Bible bashing, we need to stand firm on what we are for too. Being a Christian is often associated with rules and what we can't do, but what about all the 'benefits' of a life in Christ? What about the glorious freedom and purpose that we find in Christ? What about His provision and all the gifts of the Spirit such as peace, joy, health? Before we perish for what we are against, shall we consider perishing for what we are for?

Are you *for* the hungry and poor? When all your colleagues are talking about the stinky bum sitting outside your office, do you show compassion and the love of Christ or do you join in with the cruel remarks? Are you willing to perish in reputation and stand up for the man, offering him a kind word and perhaps a sandwich? This doesn't sound like much of a cause does it? But it IS! This man could be just one 'starfish', you simply don't know what God has planned for this man.

Every single person was perfectly designed with a destiny – EVERY SINGLE ONE of us – no exceptions. When you are making friends with one homeless, hungry person you are making friends with Jesus himself. *"Then the righteous will answer him, 'Lord, when did we see you hungry and feed you, or thirsty and give you something to drink? When did we see you a stranger and invite you in, or needing clothes and*

If I Perish, I Perish

clothe you? When did we see you sick or in prison and go to visit you?' "The King will reply, 'Truly I tell you, whatever you did for one of the least of these brothers and sisters of mine, you did for me."[58]

What cause do you stand for? Do you act self righteous around the unmarried, teenage mum you have recently met? Do you let your friends know how shocking and sinful it is so that you don't feel so bad about yourself? Do you stand against her so that you can look good and 'holy' by comparison? Or... do you stand 'for' her? Do you show her love and compassion, organise a baby shower, take her to ante-natal appointments and buy her cute things for her baby? Do you show her the love of God without even mentioning Him, just by being His hands and feet, showing His heart to her? What is your cause, are you FOR the gospel or are you living FOR yourself? Is looking good to others more important to you than making the gospel look good to those that need it? True friendship, true love is more powerful than any sermon you can preach to someone who doesn't know Jesus.

"Preach the Gospel always, and if necessary, use words." This quote, which is attributed to Francis of Assisi, is one of my favourite sayings because it's so true! Too often we want to display our knowledge of the Bible and show how spiritual

Esther or Delilah?

we are but seldom do we simply shut up, roll up our sleeves and get our hands dirty in someone else's life! I am sure when Mother Teresa, in 1948, received permission from her superiors to leave the convent school and devote herself to working among the poorest of the poor in the slums of Calcutta; she didn't have a Nobel peace prize in mind. Mother Teresa committed to loving and caring for those persons nobody was prepared to look after. She rolled up her sleeves and got her hands dirty.

Mother Teresa's work has been recognised and acclaimed throughout the world and she has received a number of awards and distinctions, including the Pope John XXIII Peace Prize (1971), the Nehru Prize for her promotion of international peace and understanding (1972), the Balzan Prize (1979) and the Templeton and Magsaysay awards. She is a legend, a woman who deeply impacted the world.

Would you like to be remembered as Mother Teresa was? Well in order to begin where she began, lose all your money and start wiping up vomit and dress loads of pussy, infected wounds in the poorest parts of the world. Do this with true love in your heart and no desire to ever be noticed or recognised. You never know, you might start an international movement or you might just become best friends with a few poor people and deeply impact their lives. Does it matter

If I Perish, I Perish

which way it goes? If it matters, then I am sorry, you are not really the 'If I perish, I perish' sort of person.

Ruth's Story

Ruth's Story

During the time of Judges, when there was a great famine in the land, an Israelite family from Bethlehem—Elimelech, his wife Naomi, and their sons Mahlon and Chilion—emigrated to the nearby country of Moab. Elimelech died, leaving Naomi and their two sons to fend for themselves.

Shortly after their father's death, both sons took wives from the Moabite women. Mahlon married Ruth and Chilion married Orpah. All seemed to go well for about ten years but then both Mahlon and Chilion died, leaving Naomi and her two daughters-in-law alone and so Naomi decided to return to Bethlehem. She very kindly told her daughters-in-law to return to their own mothers, and remarry.

 Esther or Delilah?

It was a very emotional time where the three women had to decide which path they would take in life. Orpah and Ruth did not want to leave Naomi but she insisted that she had nothing to offer them and that they were better off trying to find a husband and trying to rebuild their lives.

Orpah reluctantly leaves but Ruth says, "*Entreat me not to leave you, Or to turn back from following after you; For wherever you go, I will go; And wherever you lodge, I will lodge; Your people shall be my people, And your God, my God. Where you die, I will die, and there will I be buried. The Lord do so to me, and more also, If anything but death parts you and me.*"[59]

When Naomi saw that Ruth was determined to go with her, she stopped speaking to her and the two women returned to Bethlehem. The whole city of Bethlehem was very excited when Naomi arrived but Naomi was sad because of all she had lost.

She did however have a little hope in that she had a relative, a very wealthy family member of her husband, Boaz. It was the time of the barley harvest, and in order to support her mother-in-law and herself, Ruth goes to his fields to glean after the reapers. Boaz is kind to her because he has heard of her loyalty to her mother-in-law. Ruth tells her mother-in-law of Boaz's kindness, and she gleans in his field through the

Ruth's Story

remainder of the harvest season, enjoying the kindness and favour of Boaz to the point that he allows her to eat at his reapers table. Boaz even told the reapers to purposefully drop grain from their bundles so that Ruth could pick them up for her own use.

Naomi was thrilled to hear of all Boaz had done for Ruth and she immediately began her matchmaking scheme between Ruth and Boaz. Naomi tells Ruth to wash and wear her best garment and she then sends her to the threshing floor at night, where Boaz was eating with specific instruction. She tells Ruth to wait until Boaz has finished eating and drinking and when he lies down, to uncover his feet and to lie down by them.

Obediently, Ruth does exactly as Naomi said. Boaz awakes and asks, "Who are you?" at which point Ruth identifies herself. She then asks Boaz to take her under his wing which was a woman's way of asking for marriage.

Boaz complements Ruth for her kindness in choosing him, as he was not a young man and she had ample opportunity to pursue any of the young men in his employment. He then goes on to say, *"And now, my daughter, do not fear. I will do for you all that you request, for all the people of my town know that you are a virtuous woman."*[60]

 Esther or Delilah?

In the next sentence though, Boaz states that he is willing to "redeem" Ruth via marriage, but informs Ruth that there is another male relative who has the first right of redemption. He then says to Ruth, *"Stay this night, and in the morning it shall be that if he will perform the duty of a close relative for you—good; let him do it. But if he does not want to perform the duty for you, then I will perform the duty for you, as the Lord lives! Lie down until morning."*[61]

Ruth stayed the night so that she didn't have to walk in the dark, not because of any improper reasons. In the morning she left before anyone knew that she was there, with a sum of grain that Boaz gave her as an alibi for being out. True to his word, Boaz discussed the issue with the other male relative with the town elders present as witnesses. The other male relative is unwilling to jeopardize the inheritance of his own estate by marrying Ruth, and so relinquishes his right of redemption, thus allowing Boaz to marry Ruth.

Now this was the custom in former times in Israel concerning redeeming and exchanging, to confirm anything: one man took off his sandal and gave it to the other, and this was a confirmation in Israel.[62] And so the close relative took off his sandal and the deal was made.

Ruth's Story

Boaz and Ruth get married and immediately had a son whom they named Obed, who by Levirate customs is also considered a son or heir to Elimelech, and thus Naomi. The story is concluded by mentioning their genealogy and it is pointed out that Obed is the father of Jesse, and thus the grandfather of David which means that this is Jesus' line.

Jezebel's Story

Jezebel's Story

And it came to pass, as though it had been a trivial thing for him to walk in the sins of Jeroboam the son of Nebat, that he took as his wife Jezebel, the daughter of Ethbaal, king of the Sidonians; and he went and served Baal and worshiped him.[63]

The silly man that paid no attention to what he was doing and who did not consider the consequences of sin, was King Ahab.

Jezebel was a wealthy princess from the coastal city of Sidon in Phoenicia where her father was king. She was loyal to the gods of her family and was a zealous participant in the worship of Baal. She paid no attention to the God of Israel, Ahab's God. In fact, she massacred the prophets of the Lord and caused those left alive to flee for their lives.[64]

Esther or Delilah?

During a severe famine in Samaria, a prophet of God, Elijah, was told by God to go to present himself to Ahab. God said to Elijah, *"Go, present yourself to Ahab, and I will send rain on the earth."*[65]

Elijah did as God said and was greeted by Ahab as the 'troubler of Israel' to which Elijah replied, *"I have not troubled Israel, but you and your father's house have, in that you have forsaken the commandments of the Lord and have followed the Baals."*[66]

Elijah continued by giving a bold command that would enrage Jezebel, saying, *"Now therefore, send and gather all Israel to me on Mount Carmel, the four hundred and fifty prophets of Baal, and the four hundred prophets of Asherah, who eat at Jezebel's table."*[67]

Once everyone was gathered, an elaborate ceremony commenced where Baal was revealed as a false god and the God of Israel revealed Himself by sending fire from heaven and consuming a sacrifice. *Now when all the people saw it, they fell on their faces; and they said, "The Lord, He is God! The Lord, He is God!" And Elijah said to them, "Seize the prophets of Baal! Do not let one of them escape!" So they seized them; and Elijah brought them down to the Brook Kishon and executed them there.*[68]

Jezebel's Story

It was a wonderful time when the people turned their hearts away from Baal and back to God. Rain came as a result and the drought ended. However, yhey did not live happily ever after.

When Jezebel heard of the dramatic showdown on Mount Carmel and of the hundreds of her priests that were slaughtered, she swore revenge, sending a messenger to Elijah, saying, *"So let the gods do to me, and more also, if I do not make your life as the life of one of them by tomorrow about this time."*[69]

Elijah went into hiding for a time.

After some time passed, Ahab needed a piece of land that lay next to the palace for a vegetable garden. He approached the owner, Naboth, and offered to buy the land from him but Naboth said, *"The Lord forbid that I should give the inheritance of my fathers to you!"*[70]

Ahab went and lay on his bed and started to sulk, he wouldn't eat his food and ended up quite depressed as a result. He behaved more like a spoiled child than a king! *But Jezebel his wife came to him, and said to him, "Why is your spirit so sullen that you eat no food?"*[71] He told her what had happened with Naboth.

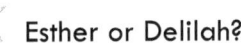 Esther or Delilah?

Jezebel decided to act. She said to him, "*You now exercise authority over Israel! Arise, eat food, and let your heart be cheerful; I will give you the vineyard of Naboth the Jezreelite.*"[72]

She ruthlessly took control of the situation and arranged the murder of Naboth so that she could take over the land that was necessary for palace expansion. *She wrote letters in Ahab's name, sealed them with his seal, and sent the letters to the elders and the nobles who were dwelling in the city with Naboth. She wrote in the letters, saying, Proclaim a fast, and seat Naboth with high honor among the people; and seat two men, scoundrels, before him to bear witness against him, saying, "You have blasphemed God and the king." Then take him out, and stone him, that he may die.*[73]

As soon as Naboth was dead, Jezebel told Ahab and he went at once to take possession of the land he wanted. Little did Ahab know what was to come as a result of his wife's actions. God spoke to Elijah and told him to go and see Ahab saying, 'Thus says the Lord: "Have you murdered and also taken possession? In the place where dogs licked the blood of Naboth, dogs shall lick your blood, even yours."'[74]

So Ahab said to Elijah, "Have you found me, O my enemy?" And he answered, "I have found you, because you have sold yourself to do evil in the sight of the Lord.[75] And

Jezebel's Story

with that Elijah reels off the huge curse that was about to be unleashed upon him. After he frightened Ahab with what was to come, he began to speak of what was to become of Jezebel saying, *"The dogs shall eat Jezebel by the wall of Jezreel. The dogs shall eat whoever belongs to Ahab and dies in the city, and the birds of the air shall eat whoever dies in the field."*[76]

Elijah continues by saying that, *"there was no one like Ahab who sold himself to do wickedness in the sight of the Lord, because Jezebel his wife stirred him up. So it was, when Ahab heard those words, that he tore his clothes and put sackcloth on his body, and fasted and lay in sackcloth, and went about mourning*[77].

Thankfully, God saw Ahab's heart and how he had humbled himself in the sight of God. God said to Elijah, *"See how Ahab has humbled himself before Me? Because he has humbled himself before Me, I will not bring the calamity in his days. In the days of his son I will bring the calamity on his house."*[78]

Ahab was spared, he was truly humbled and repentant, but Jezebel was not and so she was still in line to reap the full judgement for what she had done. It wasn't long before Ahab died in battle and after he was buried, *someone washed the chariot at a pool in Samaria, and the dogs licked*

 Esther or Delilah?

up his blood while the harlots bathed, according to the word of the Lord which He had spoken.*⁷⁹*

Jezebel had lost her husband to a noble death in battle, and then Ahaziah their son reigned in his place. He was as evil as his father and mother. *He served Baal and worshiped him, and provoked the Lord God of Israel to anger, according to all that his father had done.*⁸⁰ His reign was short and lasted only two years when he died in an 'accident', falling from through the lattice of his upper room in the palace. The details are unclear, but it is obvious there had been some sort of attempted palace coup. So Ahaziah died according to Elijah's warning and because he had no son, Jehoram, his brother, Jezebel's other son, became king in his place.

Soon another message arrived at the palace from Elijah to one of the king's commanders saying, *"You shall strike down the house of Ahab your master, that I may avenge the blood of My servants the prophets, and the blood of all the servants of the Lord, at the hand of Jezebel. For the whole house of Ahab shall perish; and I will cut off from Ahab all the males in Israel, both bond and free.*⁸¹ *The dogs shall eat Jezebel on the plot of ground at Jezreel, and there shall be none to bury her."*⁸²

And so it happened as was predicted - while Jehoram was out in his chariot he was murdered, shot in his heart with a

Jezebel's Story

bow and arrow shortly after it was said of his mother, *"What peace, as long as the harlotries of your mother Jezebel and her witchcraft are so many?"*[83]

News of her son's death quickly returned home to Jezebel. She stood in her room doing her makeup when in walked Jehu, the one who had killed her son. She hurled insults at him to which he replied, *"Who is on my side? Who?"* Immediately, two of Jezebel's eunuchs looked at him. Then he said, *"Throw her down."* So they threw her out of the window. Blood spattered on the wall as she was thrown down and fell to the pavement of the palace's central courtyard. Jehu went downstairs and ran his iron-wheeled chariot back and forth over her dying body and then went into the palace for a celebratory dinner.

Then he said, "Go now, see to this accursed woman, and bury her, for she was a king's daughter." So they went to bury her, but they found no more of her than the skull and the feet and the palms of her hands[84].

Jezebel died the most horrific death that left nothing to be buried, just as predicted; her remains were left for the dogs to eat. She had no funeral and there was no tomb stone to mark her grave.

After this, Jehu ordered the murder all of Ahab's sons, all seventy of them. Their heads were sent to Jehu in baskets

 **Esther or Delilah?**

and he ordered that they were displayed at the city gates. More killing was ordered until Jezebel, her family, and all her followers were completely wiped out.

Ruth or Jezebel?

Ruth or Jezebel?

Ruth and Jezebel, at first glance, don't seem like very different women. They are both very beautiful women, they both took control of difficult situations, both women were very adamant on certain points and both appeared to want to do what seemed right to them. As their story unfolds, the subtle differences are revealed but what is most astonishing is the fruit – the end result of their subtle differences. At times, as women, we think that the things we do or say are not really a big deal. When we act a certain way we might consider how our actions look at the time but do we consider the fruit that they will bear?

More often than not, we will look at the seed and see it as small and insignificant not realising that each seed grows into a full grown tree and will bear fruit, whether we like it or not.

 Esther or Delilah?

Many times I have observed women treating their husbands poorly. I am sure at times I am equally guilty so am by no means point any fingers here, but it is easier to see these things in someone else's life before you realise they are in yours too. On one occasion I observed a woman pointing her finger to her husband and clicking her fingers together so as to get his attention to do something for her. Her manner reminded me of how someone would instruct a dog. She is a wonderful woman in so many ways but I have observed these sorts of things and cannot help wondering what sort of fruit this treatment might bear in their marriage some day.

On another occasion I have witnessed a woman repeatedly insult her husband in front of other people. In fact I have never heard her say a kind word about her husband more than twice in all the years I have known her. Let me tell you something, the fruit in her husband is already showing and it is not a pretty sight. If ever I saw a disabled man who has been robbed of his spiritual destiny through unforgiving words, it is him.

Now don't sit there saying that you would never do that to your husband. You probably wouldn't and neither would I but I can guarantee you that there is something both in your life and mine that is equally shameful and shows disrespect to our husbands. We will only see it for what it is if we want

Ruth or Jezebel?

to see it. I try my best to observe myself and look out for little things that disrespect my husband and as soon as I find them, I make sure that I eradicate them from our marriage.

In today's society much is acceptable. By comparison to ungodly women, our behaviour probably looks impeccable as pretty much anything goes today. However, other women should not be our measure. As it says in Psalms, *"Your word is a lamp to my feet and a light to my path.*[85]*"* Our only guide should be God's word on things, which is the Bible. It is in the Bible where we can find examples of women such as Ruth and Jezebel, that we can learn from.

Do not be deceived: God cannot be mocked. A person reaps what he sows.[86] Ruth and Jezebel both planted seemingly insignificant small seeds; let's take a look at what they were and what crop they reaped as a result. As you read, take time to consider what seeds you are currently sowing in your life and then consider what fruit you will reap.

In fact, try to intercept the fruit before they even form by determining what tree will grow from the seed. Once again, you are faced with an opportunity to write your own history, to determine your own future and to use the power of your own free will. Predict your future by examining the seeds that you are currently sowing and then change your future by changing your seeds.

 Esther or Delilah?

Ruth's Seeds	Jezebel's Seeds
Waits	Demands
Humble	Proud
Builds her man	Breaks her man

Ruth's Tree	Jezebel's Tree
Influence	Control

Ruth's Fruit	Jezebel's Fruit
Saved her entire family line	Destroyed her entire family line

You

What about you? What seeds are you sowing right now? What tree and ultimately what fruit will result from your seeds? Jesus said, *"You will know them by their fruits. Do men gather grapes from thorn bushes or figs from thistles?"*[87] Right now, this very minute, you can tell what seeds you have sown by the fruit you are bearing.

If you want to change any aspect of your life, change it at seed level. Don't expect to make changes to your fruit, it simply doesn't work that way, you must change the seeds in order to change the fruit. You might even need to uproot something things in your life and replant them. Don't feel

Ruth or Jezebel?

that you have to accept the tree you have planted, some trees should be uprooted. If you insist of keeping something that you know in your heart needs to be uprooted don't ever expect any good fruit to come from it. Understand this principle, if it's time to uproot then get busy uprooting and see what beautiful thing God will plant in it's place.

Often people don't have the courage to uproot something for fear that all they will ever see afterwards is the massive hole where there something once was. God doesn't work that way! If you are faithful in uprooting something that is not right in your life, He is faithful to replace it with something so much better than you ever imagined in your wildest dreams.

Once, during the third month of a dating relationship, I realised that the relationship was totally wrong for me. I tried to end it but he pleaded for one last chance so I agreed. Needless to say, every day after that day for another YEAR my life was a mess. I was unhappy, I was miserable, my life wasn't looking so good, my job was affected, my relationship with God was affected. A year of my life was wasted simply by agreeing to be in a relationship that I knew was wrong for me. In the end I had to try to end it - again! This time it was so much more difficult and was EXTREMELY painful. If I had ended it when it was meant to end I would have saved myself a great deal of time and pain.

Eric, my husband, was the best thing that ever happened to me and I am so grateful to God for giving him to me. Looking back I can see that I was willing to settle for a life that was second best just because I didn't want to be alone. Thankfully God knew that He had Eric planned for me so that we could enjoy the most amazing life together. I shudder to think what would have happened to me if I had not uprooted that wrong relationship – I would have missed out on building the AMAZING life that I have with Eric today.

Please I beg you, don't allow nonsense to grow in your life. If you see it is wrong pull it up and if it is something that you can't uproot, ask God to help you with sorting it out. Whatever you do, don't settle for second best in any area of your life. Sometimes uprooting something is extremely difficult, especially if you have had it in your life for a very long time. I can tell you from personal experience though that it's not worth leaving it to further destroy you, uproot it and see what God will build in it's place.

He won't disappoint you. He will totally blow you away. The only reason I had the courage to uproot that unhealthy relationship was because I had God to help me to tug at it, I don't think I would have had the strength to do it on my own.

Ruth or Jezebel?

Perhaps you do not have the strength to uproot things in your life, ask God and He will give you what you need. All He needs from you is your decision and your permission for His help.

After uprooting something big like a relationship you might need a rest. Take time to heal. It would be very foolish to jump straight into another relationship before you have healed. Rest after a broken relationship is ESSENTIAL.

Other things that might need to be uprooted might be anger, bad attitudes, rebellion and hatred – all things that can be found in a marriage. Don't sit there thinking, 'that's not me', yes it might be you. It is quite possible that you have most if not all these traits in you. Think of all the times you react in anger rather than respond in love, a fruit is not easily grown but if the right seeds are sown, such as patience, kindness and love, it is possible. Count to ten before you react and before you know it, your reaction turns to a much more acceptable response. If we truly want to have the fruit of a Ruth we need to sow the seeds that Ruth sowed. Read the story of Ruth in the Bible and see what gems you can apply to your own life. Take some time to reflect on your life and fill in your own table.

Esther or Delilah?

Your Seeds

NOW   **FUTURE**

Your Tree

NOW   **FUTURE**

Your Fruit

NOW   **FUTURE**

Ruth or Jezebel?

M2M

Men, you can't blame your wife if she influences your decisions. She might bring suggestions to you or even try and take over a decision but the responsibility is on you to lead and the judgement for a bad decision will be on your head. Jezebel's husband, Ahab, was punished because of what she did. Even though Ahab had nothing to do with it, he was judged for what he left in her hands.

Firstly, Ahab allowed Jezebel to influence his faith. He did not stand firm in this area. Men, you need to lead your family in God's ways, don't lean on your wife in this area - lead the way because if anything goes wrong, God will hold you accountable and the consequences will be on you and your family. You cannot stand before God, just as Adam did, and point the finger at her, it won't work.

Secondly, learn from Ahab's mistakes. He allowed his wife to take control of a situation while he remained passive and oblivious to what she was up to. She said to him, *"You now exercise authority over Israel! Arise, eat food, and let your heart be cheerful; I will give you the vineyard of Naboth the Jezreelite."*[88] God's response to Ahab, through Elijah the prophet, was *"I have found you, because you have sold yourself to do evil in the sight of the Lord."*[89]

 ### Esther or Delilah?

Even though Ahab did not execute the plan but merely allowed his wife to get on with it, he was judged. Are you letting your wife get on with something because you can't be bothered to get involved? You may reap the judgement of her actions, so it is best to get involved and lead the way so that she doesn't feel compelled to find her own way forward. A passive man will never win, Adam lost, Ahab lost and so did many other men who didn't take the lead in the relationship. What sort of man are you?

Patience

Patience

There is something about patience. It is a beautiful quality and when you meet a patient person it is as if you can assume a whole lot of other good things about them too. Jesus said, *"By your patience possess your souls."*[90]

There is power in patience. Many times we perceive patient people to be weak people but it's quite the contrary, patient people are powerful. In James it says, *"But let patience have its perfect work, that you may be perfect and complete, lacking nothing."*[91] Wow, that is quite something, don't you think? If we allow patience to work in our life we will be perfect, lacking nothing! That would make patience a very powerful thing indeed.

Patience produces hope. There are many verses in the Bible that teach this including Romans 15:4 which says, *"that*

Esther or Delilah?

we through the patience and comfort of the Scriptures might have hope."

Patience comes from the testing of your faith.[92] Something that we all find uncomfortable is the testing part, but when we reap the fruit of the testing, it is amazing.

As we look at this powerful yet gentle word we realise that in order to bear the fruit of an Esther and a Ruth, we need to grow a set of patience in our lives. Well, I say that because patience is a fruit of the spirit[93] and as we all know fruit grows over a period of time and is not simply given as a gift is. It is evident from the stories of all the women that we have studied that patience is a key ingredient to being an amazing and Godly woman.

Esther patiently wooed her husband the king, but Zeresh advised her husband hastily, costing him his life. Ruth patiently cared for her mother-in-law whilst Jezebel hastily took over her husband's affairs so that he could grow his vegetable garden. Ruth gained a husband but Jezebel lost her husband. Ruth gained an entire line of descendants while Jezebel's entire line of descendants was wiped out.

At first glance patience doesn't seem like such a big deal but if you compared the results of the patient women and the women that lacked patience then you will begin to appreciate the value of patience. Valuing patience and

Patience

having patience is yet another thing. Some people just seem naturally patient while others seem permanently wound up! Let's examine this word patience and see how we can grow some into our lives.

Patience according to the dictionary is endurance, staying power, persistence, tolerance and even serenity. Patience from Galatians 5:22 in the original Greek text is makrothumia – μακροθυμία - which means longanimity or long suffering. The Bible's definition of patience doesn't just mean endurance or staying power but it means calmness in the face of suffering. If we want to grow patience we will need the fertiliser of suffering. There are no short cuts, no back doors, no quick fixes and no microwave options. If we want to become an Esther or a Ruth as opposed to a Delilah or Jezebel, we need to go through the long and painful process of suffering that produces patience. There is no other way, patience is an essential ingredient to being an amazing woman of God.

Consider that annoying person at work, are they perhaps sent by God to help you grow patience? What about your teenager that is pushing you to your limits, are they actually a God given tool to answer your prayer for patience? How

 Esther or Delilah?

about that car in front of you or the many cars on the road every morning, are you a patient driver?

Do you think you are patient? Let's take a look at the opposite words of patience and see how you score. The opposite of patience is annoyed, irritated, edgy, impatient, intolerant and restive. Weigh yourself up and see if you score more of the patient descriptive words or of the impatient descriptive words. Watch yourself and listen to yourself and see for yourself who you really are. I am pretty sure that we can all work on patience as none of us are perfect yet.

Gentleness

Gentleness

Gentleness is another one of the qualities that we all desire but seldom find the time to cultivate. As with all fruit of the spirit, gentleness needs to be grown over a period of time. Gentleness goes hand in hand with patience in many ways, but unlike patience, gentleness requires less suffering. The key to gentleness is self control.

Jezebel clearly wasn't a gentle person, you can tell just by reading how she behaved. She seemed cruel, unkind, ruthless, harsh and impatient. Not the sort of qualities you would associate with a gentle person. Ruth on the other hand seemed patient and although it doesn't specifically say she was gentle you can pick up certain gentleness about her as she says her *'entreat me not to leave you'* speech. These sorts of words can't really be said harshly or in anger, she would have said them with a look of love in her eyes and with a gentle tone in her voice, don't you think?

The actual word gentleness doesn't come up much at all in the original text of the Bible. Words such as meek and soft come up in verses where in modern translations we commonly use the word gentle, such as in 1 Peter 3:4 where is says that a woman's true beauty stems from *'the ornament of a meek and quiet spirit, which is in the sight of God of great price.'* and in Proverbs 15:1 where it says that 'A soft answer turns away wrath, but a harsh word stirs up anger.'

Gentleness is so very important and takes on many forms. It is not simply the lack of harshness but it is an entire attitude towards life. Someone who is truly gentle doesn't have gentle moments, moments where they refrain from anger but they *are* gentle. That is their nature and their true character from which they will respond in most situations.

Jesus called himself *'gentle and lowly in heart'*[94] and when we look into the original text we find that he is calling himself meek and lowly in heart. Meekness means gentle with humility and when Jesus called himself lowly in heart he went to the next level of humility. Lowly in heart is the lowest level of humility, it means completely depressed and cast down. When Jesus mentioned His gentleness he used two

Gentleness

words to express humility so that it was clear how important humility is.

Gentleness is not simply a soft touch or a loving, kind word to someone. It is that and so much more. True gentleness stems from true humility, something which we cannot fake or create.

Gentleness is not a feminine quality. Jesus referred to Himself as gentle. The Bible also tells us that *'the servant of the Lord must not strive; but be gentle unto all men, apt to teach, patient'*[95] and it goes on to add another layer of gentleness by saying that *'in meekness instructing those that oppose themselves'*[96]

There is no need to feel like less of a man because you have the ability to be meek and gentle. Don't forget, Jesus also took a whip and chased out the money changers from the temple. Jesus was meek and gentle but he was not a wimp. When he needed to use his righteous anger he did it with force. Don't feel like less of a man if you are gentle or desire to be gentle. Use gentleness as a default but be firm when the situation demands it.

Gentleness is a fruit of the spirit that speaks of moral excellence, goodness and kindness. So as you can see, when the fruit of the Spirit is listed in the Bible it is listed in a way that the qualities that we need are clear and that there is no room for confusion or misinterpretation. I am quite certain that both Esther and Ruth had plenty of the fruit of the Spirit in their lives as you cannot do what they did without these fruit. Let's take a look at them and how they all link together.

The fruit of the spirit are love, joy, peace, longsuffering, gentleness, goodness, faith, meekness and temperance. In modern English, translated from the original Greek text, it could read something like this, 'Affectionately, cheerfully and peacefully suffer with moral excellence, goodness and moral convictions having humility and self control.'

That pretty much sums up the best possible form of gentleness. Cultivate the fruit of the Spirit in your life and you will have the truly gentle character that enables women such as Esther and Ruth to make history.

Abigail's Story

Abigail's Story

*I*srael was in mourning.

Samuel, a great prophet, had died.

David, in his great sadness, left all the people of Israel with a few of his men and went into the wilderness of Paran, just a few miles from the city of Carmel. It was there that David met Nabal.

Nabal was a very wealthy man but he had an unfortunate disadvantage in life and that was his name. Nabal means fool! In fact its precise meaning is stupid, wicked and a vile person[97].

Nabal had a wonderful wife, Abigail. Her name meant something quite different from Nabal's. Her name meant source of joy! *She was a woman of good understanding, and*

Esther or Delilah?

of a beautiful countenance: but the man was churlish and evil in his doings.[98]

David heard that Nabal was shearing his sheep in Carmel. He had three thousand sheep and one thousand goats. David and his men spent some time with the shepherds of Nabal's flock as they journeyed through the area. While staying with the shepherd, they protected them and their sheep from outside forces. They took nothing and did no harm to them. After some time had passed David needed some sustenance and decided to send his men to ask Nabal for some food. He instructed his men to let Nabal know of their time with his shepherds and how well he had treated them.

Then Nabal answered David's servants, and said, "Who is David, and who is the son of Jesse? There are many servants nowadays who break away each one from his master. Shall I then take my bread and my water and my meat that I have killed for my shearers, and give it to men when I do not know where they are from?"[99]

David's men returned and informed him of Nabal's response to which he replied, *"Every man gird on his sword."*[100]

What started out as a peaceful and humble request turned into a battle cry for David and his men. They would not stand by and take such an insult.

Abigail's Story

Now one of the young men told Abigail, Nabal's wife, saying, "Look, David sent messengers from the wilderness to greet our master; and he reviled them. But the men were very good to us, and we were not hurt, nor did we miss anything as long as we accompanied them, when we were in the fields. They were a wall to us both by night and day, all the time we were with them keeping the sheep. Now therefore, know and consider what you will do, for harm is determined against our master and against all his household. For he is such a scoundrel that one cannot speak to him."[101]

As soon as Abigail heard of her husband's atrocious behaviour toward David, she began to make plans to make up for his foolish actions. It seems she understood the principle of 'the way to a man's heart is through his stomach' as she prepared a great deal of food and drink for David and his men. She *took two hundred loaves of bread, two skins of wine, five sheep already dressed, five seahs of roasted grain, one hundred clusters of raisins, and two hundred cakes of figs, and loaded them on donkeys*[102]. She didn't tell her husband of her plans and she and her servants journeyed to where David was and presented him with the gift of food.

As Abigail approached David she could see he was very upset. David greeted her with, *"Surely in vain I have protected all that this fellow has in the wilderness, so that*

Esther or Delilah?

nothing was missed of all that belongs to him. And he has repaid me evil for good. May God do so, and more also, to the enemies of David, if I leave one male of all who belong to him by morning light."[103]

Abigail knew she did not have a second to lose; *she dismounted quickly from the donkey, fell on her face before David, and bowed down to the ground*[104]. Immediately she took the blame for her husband's wrong doing and asked David to put the blame on her. She begged David not to regard her foolish husband, telling David what a scoundrel Nabal was saying, *"For as his name is, so is he: Nabal is his name, and folly is with him!"*[105]

She quickly explained that she had not seen David and his men and would never have allowed such treatment. Her plentiful gift was presented to David and she communicated how sorry she truly was with this poor treatment. She continued to honour David, saying good things about him and asking him to forgive her for what had happened. Abigail took full responsibility for her husband's actions and asked forgiveness accordingly. She humbled herself and interceded intensely for her people before David.

David's anger subsided and his heart softened towards Abigail. He received Abigail's gift and thanked her for meeting him. He also thanked her for her advice and

Abigail's Story

acknowledged that she had saved them all from unnecessary bloodshed that day. Finally, he concluded with, *"For indeed, as the Lord God of Israel lives, who has kept me back from hurting you, unless you had hurried and come to meet me, surely by morning light no males would have been left to Nabal!"*[106]

David thanked Abigail and let her know that he heard what she had to say, he acted on what she said and he greatly respected her as a person. After their warm exchange of words, he blessed her and told her to go up in peace to her house as she did not need to worry any more about the consequences of her husband's despicable actions.

Abigail departed from David and his men and went to see her husband. She found Nabal at home having a big party. He was drunk. Seeing him in this state, she realised that talking to him would be pointless, she did not tell him any of what had transpired between her and David until the following morning. *So it was, in the morning, when the wine had gone from Nabal, and his wife had told him these things, that his heart died within him, and he became like a stone. Then it happened, after about ten days, that the Lord struck Nabal, and he died.*[107]

It wasn't long before David heard of Nabal's death and was thrilled to bits that God had vengeance on Nabal rather

 Esther or Delilah?

than allowing David to take matters into his own hands. He recognised that he would have been evil if he had done what he intended to but that Abigail's action had prevented this great disaster. He saw that the Lord had returned the wickedness of Nabal on his own head.

David immediately sent for Abigail and proposed to her. She accepted and hurried to be at his side.

Courage

Courage

There is something about riding on a donkey into a mountain ravine and approaching four hundred angry men with swords. Not just anyone could or would do that. It takes courage.

Abigail was a woman of courage, a woman who observed an injustice and took responsibility for it. She could have left it. Her husband was a horrible man and she didn't need to protect him. In fact if David had killed Nabal she would have been free from her evil husband.

Abigail would not have been wrong if she didn't intervene. But she did.

She risked her life in several ways. Firstly, the culture of the times indicated that Abigail was Nabal's possession and her decision not to tell her husband of her plans could have

Esther or Delilah?

cost her life. He had the power to take away everything that she owned including her own life. But Abigail was a courageous woman and she didn't even consider herself, she only tried to plead for the lives of others and was prepared to die for them.

Secondly, she did not know David or his men so she could not predict his response. It was entirely possible that David and his men could have killed Abigail when she approached them. She did not see this as a reason not to go ahead, she was determined to stand in the gap for her people and her courage saved their lives.

What about you? Has God called you to take a courageous step? Are you willing to risk your life? Perhaps God is not asking you to risk your life but only your pride. Do you not say anything about the injustice at your child's school for fear of what people might think? Consider that you may need to be an Abigail, to risk certain things and use courage in order to save people. Children in schools are crying out for Christian parents to rise up. Oppressed women stuck in a sex trafficking ring are desperate for courageous women to intercede for them, perhaps even use their courage to do something for them.

Courageous women are few and far between these days, we are all waiting for someone else to do it. Women

Courage

complain about the injustice of our time but do little about it. Women gossip about other women but don't dare have the courage to talk to them face to face. Women use their husband and children as an excuse to stay in the comfort of their own home rather than get busy with fighting for a cause.

M2M Men, is your woman covering up for your mistakes? Is she taking the fall for your short comings? Is she suffering because you are leaning on her courage? You might be blessed with an Abigail but that doesn't mean you have to be a Nabal. Carefully take stock of your own life and make sure that your wife isn't living a life of covering up the mess you make.

If you recognise that this is the case, why not apologise to her and tell her how grateful you are for her courage? Most importantly, relieve her of the need to continue covering for you. Let her know that you are fully aware of the problem and are committed to working on it.

Abigail was a beautiful woman who knew how to use her beauty. She used what she had to win the favour of the leader of a nation, a king! She didn't use her husband as an excuse, saying that if she didn't tell to her husband she could

Esther or Delilah?

die. I remember doing something quite similar and although it didn't save a nation it took all my courage to do what I believed to be right. Like Abigail, I too did not tell my husband my plans as I knew he would not agree.

Let me tell you my story. I was working as a child minder. She was a single mum. I had gone out of my way to take care of her and her daughter to support her as she was trying to build her life by doing a degree at university. During the day time I took her daughter to school, fetched her from school, cooked her dinner and even took her out with my own children on family outings during the school holidays. I chose to love her daughter and treated her as my own child.

To help her out financially, I significantly reduced my child minding fees so that she didn't have to pay anything above the grant that she received for her child care. To be honest, I went way above and beyond what any child minder would have done. It was a job after all and her child was no piece of cake. She was nine years old and full of energy.

As summer approached a strange feeling began to grow in my heart. I started to get the feeling that she wasn't going to pay her child minding fees over the summer. You see, I had calculated an annual fee for her to submit for her university grant application. To make things easier for her, I took the annual fee and divided it by twelve to give her twelve easy

Courage

monthly payments. During the summer she wasn't attending university, and so therefore I wasn't required to care for her child. You can see where this is going can't you? I became increasingly concerned that she didn't plan on paying me, so I mentioned the fees to her in a subtle way.

Well what happened next was something straight from a reality TV show. She went nuts and accused me of all sorts of horrible things. After much viciousness, she said that she will not be bringing her daughter back to me ever again and will find another child minder immediately. After storming out of my home and slamming the door, she left me quite shaken. My hands and legs were trembling in a way that I had not ever experienced before and I was quite frightened at my state. I called Eric and relayed the story to him and he went nuts about what she had done to me too.

What happened next is a bit hazy but needless to say I was devastated. Not only had I lost my income for the summer and the foreseeable future, but I had lost someone I had considered a family member and a dear friend. I was grieved. The way I was treated left me deeply hurt, especially after all that I had done for her and her daughters. A few weeks passed but I continued to grieve and feel the hole in my heart growing.

Esther or Delilah?

One thing played on my mind. She was not a Christian. I had worked hard at building a relationship with her so that I could win her to Christ. Up to the point of the argument, we had become quite good friends. Despite my hurt I knew that I had to do whatever I could to restore the friendship for the sake of her salvation. This was not about me, it was about her and her eternity. I mentioned this to Eric but he was not happy with my way of thinking. He was more inclined to take her to court to claim the money that was rightfully mine.

Early one morning, 2am to be precise, I woke up with an entire email composed in my mind. It was an email to her offering an apology for the misunderstanding and asking for her forgiveness. I would tell her that she didn't owe me anything and that I wanted to stay friends with her. I quickly got out of bed, typed it up and sent it. I didn't hesitate and I didn't wake Eric to ask his opinion – I knew what he would have said anyway. It was painful to type as I humbled myself and took the blame for something that I did not do. I knew in my heart it was the right thing to do but that didn't make it hurt any less.

I pressed the send button and watched the email leave my outbox. My hole in my heart began to close, the email had been sent and the money released. I went back to sleep with

Courage

peace. No matter what happened next, I knew deep down inside that I had done the right thing.

It wasn't long before she got my email and came to my home offering me a big hug.

Our friendship was restored.

Eric wasn't happy that I had restored our friendship because he didn't like seeing me love someone who had hurt me so badly. In time though, he admitted that I had done the right thing. He acknowledged my courage and understood why I could not tell him of my plan to email her. He would surely have stopped me and a precious friendship would have been lost forever.

My little story doesn't save a nation but it did save a friendship. What story of courage should you be writing about right now? What cause is waiting for a leader to rise up in your community? Don't wait. Yes it is scary. Yes you will feel fear but as the saying goes, *'Feel the fear and do it anyway.'*

Faithfulness

Faithfulness

There is something about faithfulness. It sounds pretty. Abigail was a faithful woman. She was known to be a beautiful woman in appearance and countenance. That means her beauty shone from within and I am quite certain her humility and faithfulness shone brightly from within her.

So what is faithfulness exactly? Well I am glad you asked as I was hoping to get into it. Faithfulness in the dictionary means authenticity, truthfulness, true to one's word, loyalty and steadfastness. Devoted is a wonderful description of faithfulness too.

Faithfulness is a fruit of the spirit which is listed in some version as faith. Faithfulness in Galatians 5:22 comes from

Esther or Delilah?

the Greek word pistis (πίστις) which means persuasion, credence, moral conviction, belief, faith and fidelity.

Faithfulness in my understanding is something constant, something that doesn't just give up and let go. Abigail was faithful to her husband, despite his character. She was also faithful to her God and to what was right. In this day and age faithfulness is a rare and precious quality in a person. Most people give up easily, move on quickly and let go carelessly. Not much time is given to cultivating faithfulness in our lives. Most of us live in a microwave society where we are not interested if it doesn't pop in three minutes or can't be communicated in one hundred and forty characters or less. We microwave, we tweet, we run but few take the time to be faithful.

You can't be in a hurry and be faithful.

How could you, you wouldn't have time to think about what you are doing or what you truly believe in. Faithfulness doesn't divorce but takes time to work out marital issues. Faithfulness doesn't job hop but takes time to grow a career. Faithfulness doesn't church hop but takes time to build relationships and sort out misunderstandings. I cannot see how we can be in a rush and grow in faithfulness.

Faithfulness

Faithfulness involves devotion, commitment and loyalty. None of these attributes come instantly.

God honours faithfulness.

It takes courage to be faithful.

While researching for this chapter I came across such a beautiful article on this subject that I decided to leave it intact and share it as it was written. The article that follows is entitled, I Dare You to Stay Faithful by Earma Brown[108].

God is not unrighteous to forget your work and labour of love, which you have shown toward His name.
—Hebrews 6:10.

Impulsive yet faithful, focused yet sometimes double-minded, passionate but often presumptuous, all described an assistant of Jesus. When Jesus prophesied to His helpers and disciples that they would all forsake Him in His hour of trial, that young assistant, Peter, spoke the loudest, "Never! I will die with you, Lord!" Jesus, recognizing the passion and presumption in Peter, turned to him saying, "Peter, before the rooster crows the third time, you will have denied Me three times." It happened just as Jesus said it would. It's also recorded when Peter turned back, he strengthened his brothers. Peter continued through his failures to the fulfilment of his ministry. God counted him among the faithful eleven.

I sometimes see myself in Peter. Perhaps you see some of his human nature and tendencies in yourself. Remember when we were children and someone came up to you saying, "I dare you..." For me it didn't matter who it was, friend or foe, those words started my blood to boil and I had to complete the dare. Of course, as the word got around that characteristic did not serve me well. In fact, it got me in a lot of trouble until I finally learned better. Well this is a good dare. I charge you with a dare to be faithful in your service to a faithful God. Join me in a mission to develop faithfulness in our lives, commitments, and ministry.

All over the world churches, businesses, and organizations are looking for faithful people, people that will sign up for the long-term. The number of faithful seems to drop to lower and lower amounts. As time passes, the numbers of marriages remaining faithful are fewer. People are known to have two and three careers in a lifetime, as opposed to the twenty and thirty year tenures. Much of this has to do with the changing climate of our society. My opinion is the

Faithfulness

abounding sin in our nation and world today has an even greater impact. Yet, there's hope for this bleak picture, the writer of Romans says, where sin abounds that much more does grace abound. Furthermore, our Father God has given us the ability and the command to be faithful.

Satan is an enemy to our faithfulness. He hates it when we are faithful. I think because it reflects a faithful God to a faithless world. Therefore, it is no surprise when he sets traps and distractions to draw us from our God-ordained path. In our case, he wants to divert us from our path of service. Beware of these baits and traps of Satan:

Offenses are the bait of Satan to get one off the path of faithfulness in God. Faithfulness resists offenses. Satan will seek to trap you in unforgiveness toward a person. However, remember we always have a choice; we can be offended or forgive. Forgiveness is the right choice. Be alert to this trap because most people that have been trapped do not even realize it. Stay in tune with the Holy Spirit, for He will point out any baits of Satan making sure you are aware to make the right choice.

Pride can be very subtle in its diversion. I found myself listening to a woman confessing her discovery of pride in her life. She admitted to saying to her leader, "I have a degree in engineering and I am not going to continue in my volunteering in the Church if all you have for me to do is collating and copying." She later repented and continued faithfully helping wherever she was needed. When we are attentive to the Holy Spirit and careful to judge ourselves concerning pride, we will never be on the outside of the call and destiny God has planned for us.

Laziness and selfishness are twin enemies to the development of God's faithfulness in our life. Allowing negative emotions and feelings to dictate our behaviour rather than commitment will result in laziness. "I don't feel like it tonight. My leader will just have to make it without me…" is a common and selfish train of thought. When our fleshly desires threaten to rise up and take control, we are to offer a living sacrifice of our bodies. Then we will rise to the level of commitment we are called to as faithful servants of the most high God.

Faithfulness

Impatience is a sure enemy to faithfulness. My friends who I mentioned in an earlier chapter grew weary of waiting for their appointed leader to acknowledge their gifts and talents. They felt they should have been recommended for leadership. They did not want to hear my advice of, "I'm sure it will happen in God's timing. You are excellent candidates for leadership..." They replied, "Posh! God already knows about us and we are giving our leader six months to recognize us; if not, we are out of here." Their leader did not, and they left. Later, they came back, admitted they were wrong, and should have waited. The writer of Hebrews encourages us with, *"You have need of patience, and so after you have done the will of God you may receive his promise."*

God's faithfulness is our shield and rampart. Yet, He has commanded His ministers (those entrusted with the secret things of God) to be faithful. The Bible puts it this way, "God is looking throughout the land to find someone with their heart fully committed to Him to show Himself strong on their behalf."[109] Here are a few qualities that will nurture faithfulness in your life and ministry:

Esther or Delilah?

Develop loyalty - Form a covenant relationship with your leader. Doing so will create an allegiance that will move heaven and earth on behalf of others and yourselves.

Perseverance - The storms of life will come to any ministry. The writer of Joshua describes a scene during Joshua's life and ministry. The people of God were wavering in their decision to serve God wholeheartedly. Joshua put a clear choice before them saying, "Choose this day whom you will serve. Choose life or death." Determine like Joshua when tough times came to their ministry, "As for me and my house, we will serve the Lord."

Love much - Years ago, I was on my knees crying to my God because two good friends who started out faithful at the same time I did had backslidden in their Christianity. I was distraught because I wondered if they could go back, perhaps something could happen and I would go back to a life of sin. With tears, I said, "Lord, don't ever let me go, I love you so much…" He comforted me and gave me peace with these words,

Faithfulness

"Many have come, some will go, but you will stay. Let love be your reason for faithfulness."

Faithfulness can be considered as longevity. Faithfulness is staying for the long haul. Fulfilling our commitment accomplishes faithfulness. It takes courage to be faithful. It takes stamina to swim upstream when many are drifting downstream. God honours faithfulness in any service to Him. Buddy Bell, in his Ministry of Helps handbook says, "God called my faithfulness—my crowbar, and then commanded me to use it." Our God is one who remembers the righteous and faithful to a thousand generations.

Proverbs 31

Proverbs 31

There is something about a beautiful woman. A beautiful woman will always catch the eye of a man. A truly beautiful woman will also catch the attention of his heart. A Godly, beautiful woman will even catch the attention of other women, inspiring them to be beautiful too. Let's start this chapter near the end of Proverbs 31 which says, *"Charm is deceitful and beauty is passing, But a woman who fears the Lord, she shall be praised"*.

All the women we have studied were beautiful women but not all of them were praised. Some feared the Lord and some didn't. The results were blatantly obvious, in fact after studying these women and observing the clear pattern of the Godly women and the ungodly women, we would be foolish

Esther or Delilah?

to ever be satisfied with ungodliness ever again. Perhaps you are reading this book and you are a Godly woman or a Godly man even. Perhaps you have soaked up these words and have taken what you need to grow as a Christian. If that is the case may God richly bless you as you continue on your journey closer to Him.

Others of you may not quite know what I am talking about. You have read the words of this book, also found interesting tips but you know that you do not have the same Spirit that the Godly women in this book had. You know of God, you have heard of Jesus but you do not have a personal relationship with Him. To be truly beautiful, you need to glow with something special from within. Something that is not of this world. Something that you cannot even switch on yourself. Your glow needs to come from a source other than yourself.

Perhaps you feel tired?

Tired of trying so hard. Tired of trying to be good. Tired of feeling the emptiness inside of you that nothing and no one has ever been able to fill. Tired of feeling incomplete. Tired of feeling alone. Tired of the struggles of life. Tired of every day seeming so pointless. Tired of being tired.

Do you feel tired? May I tell you a secret? I have found a way out of all of that tiredness. His name is Jesus. No, not

Proverbs 31

the one who you think is waiting to catch you out. No, not the one who you think is writing down all your sins. No, not the one who looks down at you from some cross in a church building. That is not Jesus, that is man's perception of Jesus.

Jesus is a man. Jesus is God. Jesus is... well completely both and this is what He wants to say to you today, *"Come to Me, all you who labour and are heavy laden, and I will give you rest."*[110]

Jesus also says to you, *"Take My yoke upon you and learn from Me, for I am gentle and lowly in heart, and you will find rest for your souls."*[111]

Jesus is not pointing his finger at you, He is not going to remind you of all the times you have messed up and got it wrong. He is not going to look at you through a piercing slit in His eyes. Jesus is not going to reject you or turn you away.

Jesus wants to complete your beauty today.

Jesus wants to take all of that tiredness from your shoulders. He wants to remove the stress lines from your forehead. He wants to relieve you of that heavy load that you have been carrying around for so long. He wants to free you from guilt and shame.

Jesus knew that we would mess up, so He paid the fine in advance. The penalty for our mess was death, we deserved

Esther or Delilah?

the death sentence as we broke God's law. Jesus loved us so much, that He took the penalty upon Himself.

He died.

We are free. The bill is paid in full, no longer do we have to carry the heavy burden of an unpaid debt. Few people realise this which is why they are so tired. They are trying so hard to pay off a debt which has already been paid.

Are you crying right now? Are you screaming out 'yes' from deep down inside your soul? Are you wondering if this is possible or what the catch is?

There is no catch and yes it is possible.

It's simple, just tell Jesus how you feel and ask Him to come into your life. No matter what you say to Him or how you pray, He will hear your heart and come closer to You. If you want a little help with words, use the prayer that follows to help you along.

Proverbs 31

Prayer

Dear Lord Jesus,

I am tired.

I feel ugly.

I want to be a truly beautiful woman who fears the Lord. I want to know You and today I want put my life right with you. I want to be free from all the guilt and shame. I want to give my heavy load to You today. I say yes to your offer of perfect love and I gratefully receive this love now. I thank you that your death on the cross made it possible for me to be clean and to be free.

Please wash me clean today so I can have a brand new start. Please forgive me of all my past sins. Please fill me with your Holy Spirit. You are my Lord and Saviour now.

AMEN

I am so happy for you, for the decision you have just made. If you have prayed this prayer I would love to hear from you. Please get in touch at <u>angela@kingsdaughters21.co.uk</u>

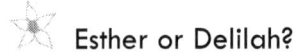 **Esther or Delilah?**

Here are some little gems from the Bible that will help you understand what has just happened to you.

Therefore, if anyone is in Christ, he is a new creation; old things have passed away; behold, all things have become new. - 2 Corinthians 5:17

As far as the east is from the west, so far has He removed our transgressions from us. – Psalms 103:12

For "whoever calls on the name of the Lord shall be saved." – Romans 10:13

For I know the thoughts that I think toward you, says the Lord, thoughts of peace and not of evil, to give you a future and a hope. – Jeremiah 29:11

We love Him because He first loved us. – 1 John 4:19

If you aren't already in a church, find a church where you feel at home and get to know people right away.

About Angela

About Angela

Angela is a mother of four, a pastor at D7 Church, author and song writer. Born in Crawley, she spent all of her childhood in South Africa and now lives in Cheltenham with her Brazilian husband, Eric.

Angela has a passion to see people reach their full potential. In particular, she has a heart to see women set free from the lies that the enemy has fed them. She has published many books which cover the issues keeping today's women from being free.

She also writes a Blog about being a 21st century princess at www.kingsdaughters21.co.uk and hosts an annual UK women's conference www.kingsdaughtersconference.co.uk

Esther or Delilah?

Other Books *by* Angela

Hope's Journey

"There was a time when all I wanted was to die but now that I have tasted life I really don't want to die until I have truly lived!" Hope's Journey is a heart wrenching account of Angela's struggle with depression & suicide.

Hope's Journey STUDY GUIDE

We all need HOPE. Hope's Journey STUDY GUIDE is about working together to find the hope that we have lost - a practical study to help you find a healthier mental, emotional and physical life for self-study or group studies.

About Angela

Secure on the Rock

Every little girl wants to know that their daddy thinks they are beautiful! As we grow older, that doesn't change, we still long to hear the words, "You are beautiful". But what if your daddy didn't call you beautiful but hurt you and did things he shouldn't?

Secure on the Rock STUDY GUIDE

We have all been through "stuff" that has robbed us of our security - it's time to take back what is rightfully ours. Secure on the Rock STUDY GUIDE is about finding security together, ideal for self-study or small group studies.

Esther or Delilah?

Passion & Purity

"God made us girls for extravagant, wild, imaginative, adventurous, fantastic loving!" Angela openly shares of how her search for passion ended up in adultery and how she managed to find a way back to purity.

Passion & Purity STUDY GUIDE

Is your marriage lacking 'spark'? Are you good friends but not passionate lovers? Get that spark back and live as God intended you to live - with extravagant, wild, imaginative, adventurous, fantastic loving!

About Angela

Being a Wife

Being a Wife is a follow on from *Being a Woman* where we go into the biblical role of the wife in depth. A refreshing read on being a wife with lively, real discussion with a group of every day ordinary women - it's NOT at all what you might think

He Restores My Soul

Do you ever feel like you are stuck on a treadmill that is set too fast and you cannot find the stop button? Modern living can often feel just like that at times. Stress, heart attacks, family breakdown and so much more is the result of the way we live our life these days. Press the pause button, take a deep breath, and uncover a much better way to live your life.

Esther or Delilah?

Free
Living life the way it was meant to be. There has to be more to life than this! What am I here for? What is my purpose? Who am I really? I have to find myself! Am I good enough? Who am I? "*Free*" explores all these nagging questions.

Nature's Way
You have the right to know that the government doesn't review the safety of products before they're sold. You have the right to practical solutions to protect yourself and your family from everyday exposures to the chemicals that modern health and beauty products contain. Exercise your rights today and begin taking care of yourself NATURE'S WAY.

About Angela

The Tale of a Church Planter

The ups, downs, frustrations, joys and everything in-between on the roller coaster ride of church planting. I can honestly say that no recipe or formula for church building exists - God does not work in this way! D7 Church is proof of this. Not because we didn't try, we did try just about everything. It was only when we gave up and said so to God that we began to have breakthrough. This is our story.

Being a Woman

"What is the true meaning of being a woman?" The heart of a woman screams to be free to love extravagantly and to live intentionally. A refreshing read with lively discussion from six women - it's NOT at all what you might think.

Esther or Delilah?

Money Matters

Are you tired of trying to get through each month, living only to make ends meet? Have you read all the books that promise 'seven steps to financial freedom' but lead you nowhere? Or are you someone who has plenty of money but can't find any satisfaction in life?

Money Matters has powerful, yet easy to understand principles that will radically revolutionise your view of money. Best of all you don't need a huge bank balance as a starting point, no matter what your current financial situation, whether rich, poor or anywhere in between, these principles will challenge you to the core resulting in financial freedom and a life of contentment GUARANTEED.

Money Matters is a set of three books that will completely revolutionise your finances. Starting with simple truths to lead you to financial freedom, followed by a devotional that will assist you in renewing your mind in the area of finances and finally a workbook that offers very practical guidelines along with spreadsheets and tools for calculating your budget.

About Angela

Money Matters

Simple Truths Leading to Financial Freedom

Money Matters Devotional

Renewing the Mind in the Area of Finances

Money Matters Workbook

Sort Out Your Money One Step at a Time

About Lorah

About Lorah

Lorah-Kelly Nell is Angela's twenty year old daughter and she has done all the graphics in *Esther or Delilah?*.

Lorah is a talented singer, photographer, artist, dress maker and also the Creative Pastor of D7 Church. She was born in Britz, South Africa but has lived in England for the past ten years. Lorah has a passion to see people lead a full and meaningful life through knowing Jesus.

For more about Lorah and all the exciting things that she does, have a look at her website and blog,
www.lorahkelly.co.uk

References

Esther's Story

[1] Esther 1:4
[2] Esther 1:5
[3] Esther 1:11-12
[4] Esther 1:13
[5] Esther 1:16-21
[6] Esther 2:2-4
[7] Esther 2:13
[8] Esther 2:15
[9] Esther 2:17
[10] Esther 3:3-5
[11] Esther 4:1
[12] Esther 4:11-12
[13] Esther 4:13-14
[14] Esther 5:1-4
[15] Esther 5:12-14
[16] Esther 6:3-6
[17] Esther 6:12-14
[18] Esther 7:7-10
[19] Esther 8:1-2

References

Delilah's Story

[20] Judges 16:5
[21] Judges 16:9
[22] Judges 16:17
[23] Judges 16:25-30

Influence

[24] Luke 12:48
[25] Esther 1:1
[26] 1 Corinthians 11:28
[27] James 1:19
[28] Proverbs 14:29
[29] 1 Peter 3:4
[30] Matthew 7:1-2

Respect

[31] John 8:7
[32] John 8:11

Submission

[33] 1 Peter 2:13-14
[34] Ephesians 5:22
[35] Ephesians 5:21
[36] Luke 22:42
[37] Isaiah 14
[38] Isaiah 55:9

Esther or Delilah?

[39] Luke 19:26
[40] Proverbs 15:1
[41] 1 Corinthians 13:8
[42] 1 Peter 3:7
[43] 2 Timothy 2:14
[44] 1 Corinthians 14:34
[45] Proverbs 27:15
[46] 1 Peter 3:4
[47] 2 Corinthians 9:7
[48] Luke 19:40
[49] Isaiah 55:12
[50] Esther 8:5
[51] 2 Timothy 2:25
[52] Proverbs 25:15

If I Perish, I Perish

[53] John 12:24
[54] Philippians 2:7 (NIV)
[55] Philippians 4:19
[56] Romans 8:28
[57] Luke 9:24
[58] Matthew 25:37-40

Ruth's Story

[59] Ruth 1:16-17
[60] Ruth 3:11
[61] Ruth 3:13

References

[62] Ruth 4:7

Jezebel's Story

[63] 1 Kings 16:31
[64] 1 Kings 18:4
[65] 1 Kings 18:1
[66] 1 Kings 18:18
[67] 1 Kings 18:19
[68] 1 Kings 18:39-40
[69] 1 Kings 19:2
[70] 1 Kings 21:3
[71] 1 Kings 21:5
[72] 1 Kings 21:7
[73] 1 Kings 21:8-10
[74] 1 Kings 21:19
[75] 1 Kings 21:20
[76] 1 Kings 21:23-24
[77] 1 Kings 21:25-26
[78] 1 Kings 21:29
[79] 1 Kings 22:38
[80] 1 Kings 22:53
[81] 2 Kings 9:7-8
[82] 2 Kings 9:7-10
[83] 2 Kings 9:22
[84] 2 Kings 9:34-35

Ruth or Jezebel?

Esther or Delilah?

[85] Psalm 119:105
[86] Galatians 6:7 (man replaced with person to indicate mankind)
[87] Matthew 7:16
[88] 1 Kings 21:7
[89] 1 Kings 21:20

Patience

[90] Luke 21:19
[91] James 1:4
[92] James 1:3
[93] Galatians 5:22

Gentleness

[94] Matthew 11:29
[95] 2 Timothy 2:24
[96] 2 Timothy 2:25

Abigail's Story

[97] From Strongs #H5037
[98] 1 Samuel 25:3
[99] 1 Samuel 25:10-11
[100] 1 Samuel 25:13
[101] 1 Samuel 25:14-17
[102] 1 Samuel 25:18
[103] 1 Samuel 25:21-22

References

[104] 1 Samuel 25:23
[105] 1 Samuel 25:25
[106] 1 Samuel 25:34
[107] 1 Samuel 25:37-38

Faithfulness

[108] Used with permission by Earma Brown, Co-Founder of Armorbearers International
[109] 2 Chronicles 16:9

Proverbs 31

[110] Matthew 11:28
[111] Matthew 11:29

Esther or Delilah?

Made in the USA
Charleston, SC
02 June 2012